Rejoice Always

Reclaiming Holy Joy In the Midst of
Suffering and Uncertainty

AMAZON #1 BESTSELLING AUTHOR

STEVE BABBITT

*Book Two of the **Fruit of the Spirit** Series*

Rejoice Always

Reclaiming Holy Joy in the Midst of Suffering and Uncertainty

ISBN-13: 978-1-7332002-2-6

Published by:
Two Tees Press
10174 Austin Drive #1845
Spring Valley, CA 91977

Editor: Lauren Mix of LM Editing
www.LMeditingservices.com / LMeditservices@gmail.com
603-660-9090

Book/Cover Design Concept: Tamara Parsons
Kensington Type & Graphics | www.kentype.com

DEDICATION

Dedicated to
Jay Lovelass
and
Emma Sinford
whose joy is now complete.

TABLE OF CONTENTS

Fruit First

About The Fruits of the Spirit Series

So much of what Christians busy themselves with today, in the name of Jesus, has very little to do with what He desired of His followers. We simmer with religious activity and fill our existence with tokenized rituals that hardly leave room for Jesus.

His desire? That we simply abide in Him, as branches in the vine, and that through the joy of abiding in Him, we bear fruit that blesses both God and our neighbors.

Drawing inspiration from the "Fruits of the Spirit" enumerated in Galatians 5 (love, joy, peace, patience, kindness, goodness, faith, gentleness, and self-control), this series is devoted to cultivating such fruit in the life of a believer.

In these meditations and sermons on the Fruit of the Spirit, Christians will be challenged to measure spiritual success the way Jesus did — not according to religious busywork but according to the blossoming fruitfulness of our lives as we walk in the Spirit.

May you both **be blessed** and **be a blessing** as you read!

"You make known to me the path of life;
in your presence there is fullness of joy;"
(Psalm 16:11)

FOREWORD:
CINDY HOFFMAN

Twenty-two years ago, one phone conversation with a young pastor had a profound impact on my life and the lives of my children. At that time, I was a single parent, not by choice but because of a horrible set of circumstances which necessitated a move from Clark County, Nevada to San Diego County, California. In anticipation of the move, I made some calls to local churches to inquire into their ministry and decide which I should visit. Steve Babbitt returned one of my phone calls and has been my friend ever since.

Our family liked him immediately, especially my son, Jeremiah, who we all call Jay. Jay was a unique person with a gentle soul who struggled with his Duchenne Muscular Dystrophy diagnosis. Steve became a tireless champion for my son with special health needs and became an advocate for our family. Steve and Jay seemed to connect on a deep level as there were words Jay could not voice that Steve could hear in his heart. It's my privilege to know Steve and his wonderful wife, Tammie, and have been asked to write this foreword.

Steve's book is about joy. He's qualified to write about the subject due to his experiences with people of varying age, gender, ethnicities, nationalities, vocations, and socioeconomic status through his work in the private sector, his role as a pastor in an economically depressed area, his mission work, his outreach within youth ministry, and the various volunteer work and community outreach projects he has led or been instrumental in making a success. Through these work and personal contacts, he's learned, first-hand, of suffering and observing joy in people who often appear, at first glance, not to have much to be joyful about.

Jay knew joy. He knew joy even when his own father disappointed him with his inconsistent presence. He knew joy even when excluded by others due to being differently abled. He knew joy even when he realized the limitations of his neuromuscular disease. He knew joy despite a life so frequently full of sorrow and profound sadness as he contemplated dying.

What was the source of his joy? Was it because he had health, wealth, family, good friends, courage, a sense of humor and a contagious smile? No, it was none of those things. He had hope because he had a personal relationship with Christ and accepted the free gift of salvation and joyfully completed believer's baptism. Just 6 months later he went to be with his Heavenly Father. His life verse is one we can all adopt.

"For I know the plans I have for you,"
declares the Lord,
"plans to prosper you and not to harm you,
plans to give you hope and a future."
(Jeremiah 29:11)

The joyful hope in this verse gave him courage to hold on when he needed to fight and the peace to let go when it was time. Steve Babbitt has perfectly captured the essence of my son Jay and others in his book. I highly recommend reading this book, which defines and answers the question, what is joy?

Cindy Hoffman
Mother of Jay Lovelass

FOREWORD:
Kristin Hetrick

I first knew Steve Babbitt as a fellow parent of a child with cystic fibrosis, then also as a friend and pastor and, now, as an author.

Having my daughter, Emma, be a part of this book on joy was an honor because I knew my daughter as one of the most joyful people I'd ever known, and to learn that others also saw her this way touched me deeply.

Emma was a child of God and shared His love not only with her words but with her actions. Even when she was beating Steve's son, James, at Battleship (over FaceTime) or having a dance off with James and his younger brother John outside of the windows of their respective hospital rooms, she rejoiced and loved her friends deeply. I know she knew her time here on earth was short, and she seemed to soak it all in.

I spent many meals and conversations at the Ronald McDonald House with Steve, and our kids played many rounds of, the now infamous game, "Kicker Ball" on the 2nd floor of the Rose Pavilion courtyard, one of the few places Emma and James could be near each other but not too close. There, or on the zipline Steve built in their backyard. I have been so blessed to have those moments where our families could be together. Whether sharing carpool with our other kids or showing up when the other was in the hospital on "duty" needing some support, I am thankful to know Steve and Tammie and the rest of the Babbitts.

I hope you find joy in the words written and memories shared in this book.

"Rejoice always,
pray continually,
give thanks in all circumstances;
for this is God's will for you in Christ Jesus."
(1 Thessalonians 5:16-18)

Kristin Hetrick
Mother of Emma Sinford

REV. SCOTT ARCHER

Steve and Tammie Babbitt, dearest friends to my wife and me for over 25 years, are possibly the most joy-full people I know. And as Steve elucidates in this excellent book, the Babbitt's joy, rather than being superficial and circumstantial, has been tested and proven through the real-life furnace of deep disappointment, disillusionment and despair. I have had the privilege of walking with Steve through some of the darkest moments of his life and have witnessed firsthand as he and Tammie have wrenched joy from the jaws of despair by crying out to God and clinging to Jesus. Whatever difficulty you find yourself in today, Steve's personal stories and biblical insights will challenge you, encourage you and guide you to discover the depths of God's love and care for you in Christ Jesus and to develop a genuine joy that is truly invincible.

Scott Archer
Senior Pastor
Central Congregational Church
La Mesa, California

INTRODUCTION

"Rejoice in the Lord always; again I will say, rejoice.
Let your reasonableness be known to everyone.
The Lord is at hand; do not be anxious about anything,
but in everything by prayer and supplication
with thanksgiving let your requests
be made known to God.
And the peace of God,
which surpasses all understanding,
will guard your hearts and your minds
in Christ Jesus."
(Philippians 4:4-7)

Most of us would like to be happy all the time. Yet problems arise, pain persists, and distractions abound. In a world where we oscillate between troubles we can't control and short-lived amusements, unshakable joy — what I call **holy joy** — can be hard to find.

Revolutionary Joy

Just the same, the Apostle Paul gives his friends in the faith the most curious command in 1Thessalonians 5:16 — *"Rejoice always."*

He issues the same decree again in Philippians 4:4, this time with an important nuance: *"Rejoice **in the Lord** always — again I say rejoice!"*

How can someone as bright as Paul put forth such a pollyannaish challenge as *"rejoice always"*? He knew the people he was writing to were suffering. Either Paul was wildly ignorant of the human condition, or he was really onto something big.

We could argue that Paul was out of touch with reality —
if he wasn't so prone to serious rejection and suffering himself.
The man who uttered those seemingly insanely happy words,
"Rejoice always," had been flogged, imprisoned, tortured, re-
jected, and disowned — he even had a bounty on his head!

Still, we find Paul, at various times in the New Testament,
either singing worship songs from his cold, dark dungeon in
Philippi, or penning astonishing words of encouragement to
friends being persecuted while he himself endured horrific tor-
ture.

If anyone had the authority to challenge us to rejoice in the
midst of trials, it was Paul! No stranger to severe suffering, Paul
speaks from experience when he calls on us to shatter the iron
sky of our present troubles with the rod of eternal joy.

What's Wrong with Our Joy?

One of the reasons we find it so hard to accept Paul's in-
structions to "rejoice always" is because we look for lasting joy
in sources that are ultimately lacking.

We starve ourselves of real joy by serially consuming the
empty calories of temporary, earthly power-ups. Meanwhile, we
fail to address our deeper need for lasting joy that never fails. Is
it any wonder that those who have spent a lifetime in pursuit of
temporary happiness in the form of sex, money, and entertainment find themselves deeply depressed by the unending emptiness inside?

Invincible joy requires an invincible source. That source is
the invincible love of God.

The key to developing and maintaining holy joy isn't com-
plicated. It simply requires that we keep our minds on Heaven
instead of the world. To put it another way, if we remind ourselves that the end of the story is far more important than the
middle, we can "count it all joy" even when the daily plotline
twists toward trouble or the quick flush of temporary amusements leaves us aching for something more real.

Alive Among the Dead

Several years ago, on a family vacation in eastern Canada, my brother in-law, Robert Yeider, and I stumbled across the ruins of a pioneer cemetery. Hiking along the dirt trail, we almost missed the headstones, barely visible through the stand of old woods and dense tree pattern. There was no mistaking the faint outline of a small, long-forgotten burial ground. We scouted the edges and found the fading remnants of approximately twenty sandstone monuments in neat rows, spaced six feet apart. The weathering of time had rendered the grave markers hopelessly unreadable except for a deep cross etched into several of the slabs.

Who were these people? What were their names? What had they lived for? And why did no one seem to remember or care about their chalky bones, slipping slowly away beneath the overgrowth of time?

This caused me to reflect on our own state of being, our bodies not the only things about us in a constant state of decomposition. Our minds, too, deteriorate. Whatever wealth we have accumulated is always evaporating, evidence of our accomplishments slowly being forgotten. In less than one hundred years from now, many of us will be gone, leaving behind only the material things, the cheap imitations of substance that provided us with temporary joy. These pleasures of the world may, indeed, burn brightly but only for a few moments before the hot glow dissipates, once again, into the cold darkness of our final, and ultimately forgotten, resting place.

So, what is **most real** about us? Are we more than our bodies? Our minds? Are we more than our achievements or possessions? Where can we find true joy, if every joy the world has to offer seems destined to slip beneath the underbrush?

Don't misunderstand me. I am not saying that the temporary joys of the body, mind, material world, or our achievements aren't real — only that they are **less real** than the lasting joy found when we walk in the Spirit. There is nothing wrong with enjoying a nice meal with your family, reading a good book, or painting a pretty picture. In the right context, these are gifts from God that we are meant to enjoy. They are not inherently wrong, only inherently *temporary*. However, even the most wholesome, noble temporary joys we experience can distract us from the greatest joy.

If we want to find lasting joy, we must look in lasting places.

Some might say, along with the author of the Bible book Ecclesiastes, that the best we can do to find joy is work, eat, drink, and be merry: pursuing earthly pleasure after earthly pleasure to keep the buzz going.

As appealing as this idea sounds at first, eventually we realize that human appetites for pleasure only grow more voracious over time, leading us into a widening spiral of ever more risky and destructive choices. The pursuit of temporary, false joys ultimately leaves us no better off than an addict whose first high is always regarded as the best. No matter how much they stab their cravings with their steely knives, they can't kill the beast that pursues that first experience with "one more hit". Ironically, seeking temporary joy after temporary joy can produce some of life's deepest sorrows.

This Dullard's Cycle simply cannot be the best we can do in our quest to find lasting joy.

Ask a Dying Person

Ana Stenzel, a brave young woman who passed away after a heroic, lifelong struggle against cystic fibrosis, shared this wisdom: "By living alongside death for so long, I have truly lived. By being aware of that limited time, I have not wasted any time, and my life has been better for it."

Dying people — particularly those with faith — often do not face death with fear but with joy. Those around them are stricken with anxiety while they bask in billows of peace. How is that? I believe it is because our brothers and sisters with a terminal illness are aware that *they are playing a much longer game*. They look beyond the short game of their bodily decay, seeing past the emptiness of temporary health in this life, and hold fast to the hope that an incredible party is going on just beyond the paper walls of earth.

Consequently, those who understand that joy in this life is fleeting are less distracted by the charms of the world. Thus, they are apt to experience real joy — a joy that can be found only when playing the long game of eternity.

When we stop pinning our happiness on tangible things and start reaching out to the intangible, taste the sweetness of a higher goodness, and hear the still, small voice of God, we discover a joy that nothing in this world can compete with.

"Think of life as a terminal illness, because if you do, you will live it with joy and passion, as it ought to be lived," writes Anna Quindlen in *A Short Guide to a Happy Life.*

This book is about joy — ***real joy***, the second fruit of the Spirit found in Galatians 5:22-23. We will explore the long game of real joy in the chapters that follow and learn to pursue it wholeheartedly, even as the world howls at our heels to invest everything in its dodgy portfolio of fleeting joys.

Later chapters will expose one of the world's false joys, examine the underlying reasons we crave it, and explore the ways Christ, alone, provides lasting joy that satisfies each hunger of the soul.

Joy or Happiness?

As you read, I will not make the typical distinction between the words "joy" (as a more spiritual, deeper, internal quality) and "happiness" (as a more superficial, externally motivated experience) in the pages that follow. While some may find it helpful to split that hair, I'm not particularly interested in belaboring an already well-documented and clever point. That ground has been covered in a gazillion books and sermons already.

If you really wanted to apply that specific rubric to what follows, my phrase "false joy" would roughly equate to their word "happiness," and what I call "holy joy" would be the equivalent of their "joy." However, it is probably best just to set any "happiness versus joy" notions aside as you read this book.

That all being said, I might use the terms "joy" and "happiness" interchangeably moving forward. In some places I might talk about "holy joy." In others, I might call it "holy happiness." I mean the same thing.

I am more concerned with recapturing the proper *source* of our happiness and joy, which is the love of God as revealed through Jesus Christ alone.

An Invitation to Holy Joy

And so, without any further delay, I invite you to read on.

If anything that follows comforts you, good!

If anything challenges you, even better.

If anything *changes* you, that is best.

CHAPTER ONE:
REASON FOR JOY

"Rejoice always"
(1 Thessalonians 5:16)

On a recent, three-day getaway with my wife, we stayed in a remote location. As is my habit, I rose early each morning to pray and read. I sat on the back porch where I had an unobstructed view of the pre-dawn sky.

The first two mornings, the stars were incredible. I could see thousands of them. On the final morning of our trip, I was eager to get one last glimpse of the starry host. I woke up extra early and headed for my usual perch only to discover that a cloud bank had rolled in, rationing the beauty to five or six stars at a time through tiny breaks in the curtain between.

Instead of joy, disappointment set in. I had counted on the stars to make me glad one more time, but I couldn't see them anymore. A more mature person would have remembered that the stars were still there — they had not forsaken me. In a short time, they would all be revealed again. I realized, then, that the clouds had not robbed me of joy, rather, my own point of view was the culprit.

Joy, like love, is a long, long road. Unlike love, however, joy is not a primary element. While **love** is foundational and exists whether we recognize and participate in it, **joy** simply **does not exist apart from a source.**

Joy is a **response** to a **stimulus**. Always.

For example, when a child sees a butterfly, they experience joy. The butterfly is the stimulus; joy the response.

Following this example, happiness can be as fleeting as a

butterfly. In a moment it may disappear, and the feeling of joy — although real and sincere — will soon be gone with it.

Consider balloons as another example.

At a fair, a child may be mesmerized by colorful balloons for sale. When they are given one, they feel happy – but only for a short while. The balloon quickly loses its luster, starts to go flat, and is finally discarded. The balloon was a real stimulus that produced real joy — **but only temporarily**.

In the same way, memories also bring us joy — a particular smell, a certain place, an old photo. Such memories are the **stimulus**, and the resulting joy is the **response**.

If joy is a response, it is always the product of some other idea, thing, or person. Whether that stimulus is *external* (as with butterflies and balloons) or *internal* (as with happy memories), **the effect of joy always has a cause.**

This begs the question — What kind of **cause** can produce joy that "rejoices always"? Is there **joy that never quits?**

For followers of Jesus, our reason for *"rejoicing always"* should be clear: the **never-ending love of God**. We rejoice always because we are loved — always.

A limitless source provides limitless joy. When we seek joy elsewhere — say, for example, in balloons and butterflies — we find those joys to be **real**, but **they vanish far too quickly**.

Joy based on *temporary* things is *temporary*. Joy based on *eternal* things is *eternal*. Temporary joy is easily crushed under the weight of human suffering. Eternal joy, on the other hand, refuses to be extinguished even through the darkest night of suffering. In fact, for those who have discovered it, everlasting joy actually seems to **flourish** in the face of suffering!

Toward the end of his career, Abraham Maslow, author of the famous hierarchy of human needs (where "self-actualization" was put forward as the highest goal in life), had something of a change of heart. In the book published shortly after his death, *The Farther Reaches of Human Nature*, Maslow amended his original theory to add a higher, more motivational step beyond self-actualization. He called this critical stage "self-transcendence."

While not overtly spiritual in nature, Maslow's revised theory recognized that there was something missing in his original pyramid of needs. Sometimes people without food, shelter, and safety find deep joy and purpose. For example, political prisoners might be more inspired after they are tortured. Children living through war still play games. Caged birds still choose to sing. How can this be?

In Maslow's opinion, it is because we have a deeper human need for transcendence or "big picture" perspective. Here's what I think he meant: if my perspective is limited to my present problems, then I will never find lasting happiness. But if I can step back and see my life from a cosmic perspective, all of my present suffering matters very little. More important than safety, or even food, or shelter, Maslow eventually argued, is the need to see ourselves as part of something bigger than our present circumstances and suffering.

While Maslow never articulated it this way, I am convinced that what he was talking about is our need for God.

What we need, in order to be able to "rejoice always" is a *source* of joy that is "always on" — a reason that is *even more real* — than the temporary stimuli that bring us short-term joy.

We are on the hunt for a joy that is foundationally different from the limited joys the world has to offer.

Because we are exploring the fruit of the Spirit (as opposed to fruit of the flesh), and because our happiness is therefore rooted in a God who is holy, I will call this lasting "always joy", *holy joy*.

The joy a beloved child of God experiences is beyond any of the false joys the world has to offer and deserves a name that transcends the limitations of humanity. It is different. It is special. It is *sacred*.

There is no better way to describe "always joy" than "holy joy."

There is *earthly joy* — and there is *holy joy*.

Holy joy — the most *real* joy — is being happy, not because we have money in the bank but because we know that our security and provision comes from a God who abundantly supplies all we need.

Holy joy — the most *true* joy — is being happy, not because we look good in the mirror but because we know that we are truly loved — no matter how we look or feel.

Holy joy — the most *lasting* joy — is not found in piling-on heady knowledge but in **being known** and piled-on with God's love.

> *This is what the Lord says:*
> *"Let not the wise boast of their wisdom*
> *or the strong boast of their strength*
> *or the rich boast of their riches,*
> *but let the one who boasts boast about this:*
> *that they have the understanding to know me,*
> *that I am the Lord, who exercises kindness,*
> *justice and righteousness on earth,*
> *for in these I delight,"*
> *declares the Lord.*
> *(Jeremiah 9:23-24)*

The false joy afforded by riches is limited and contingent.

The false joy offered by health or beauty is ultimately diminished.

The false joy granted to nimble minds eventually becomes unreliable.

But the source of holy joy — ***the love of God*** — never fails.

Only a ***love*** that is invincible can produce **joy** that is invincible. The Father's unending, unyielding, unlimited, and unfathomable love is the believer's source of "always joy" — ***holy joy***.

If we know that He loves us, we have every reason to rejoice always.

On the other hand, if we do not know that we are loved by God, the best joy will always elude us.

Three Obstacles to Holy Joy

Three obstacles threaten to obscure our view of God's love

and separate us from experiencing holy joy: ***suffering***, ***uncertainty***, and ***false joys***.

Suffering

Suffering is like an iron veil that seeks to separate us from true joy by reminding us of our mortality. Whether it is the diagnosis of a terminal illness, active persecution, or any other reminder that we *"are destined to die once" (Hebrews 9:27)*, suffering makes even the strongest among us question whether there is any reason to rejoice ***at all***, let alone rejoice ***always***.

Yet sometimes, *we witness the miracle* of those who experience joy even when faced with certain death, and we wonder how this can be.

Suffering sparks transcendence like nothing else. What other choice do we have when faced with pain and mortality than to hope that there is something better on the other side? Perhaps, in some ways, it is easier to focus on the joy ***beyond the barricade*** when the barricade is so blunt, so bleak, and so final.

Allow me to illustrate with a story from my early years in pastoral ministry.

I was in seminary, working as a youth pastor at a wonderful church in San Diego — Faith Chapel. The lessons I learned under the leaders and in the fellowship there still speak to me daily. However, one lesson outshines them all, and it came from a young, disabled man named Jay.

Jay was a bright, joyful, and handsome middle school boy of 12 when I met him. His mother wheeled him into our busy youth group one Wednesday evening and explained to me that he had trouble walking and talking because he was suffering from Duchenne's muscular dystrophy.

Jay had no trouble at all smiling and making friends, though!

Jay (officially Jeremiah) was an immediate hit among the kids at our Vertical Reality "VR" youth group. Over the next few years, we all grew to love Jay deeply. Moreover, we all knew he loved us, even though his condition hindered his ability to verbalize his sentiment. He was not merely ***welcomed*** by the group, he **belonged** — something far too few people navigating life with a disability experience in churches.

Although his spirit was formidable, over time Jay's body weakened, and we knew his time was coming soon.

On November 11, 2001, our amazing high school pastor, Tony Orlando, and I baptized Jay (as it required two of us to carry him into the baptistry and support him). I still remember the deafening roar of the crowd that Sunday morning when Jay rose out of the water. He was, as always, contagious with **unspeakable joy**.

Only a few months later, on May 25, 2002, I sat in a 3rd floor room at Children's Hospital with his mother Cindy as she cradled his 14 year-old body in her arms. His flesh simply could go no further.

Just two weeks shy of finishing 8th grade, Jay had crossed over the barricade. His joy was complete.

Although he had no earthly reason to be, Jay was — among thousands of other wonderful attributes — a **joyful** person. If his reasons for joy had been wealth, health, or power, he would have been the least joyful among us, for he had none of those things. What he did have was the insight to **see beyond the barricade of his suffering** and into the **unending love of God**.

This is why we so often discover these remarkable people who are able to rejoice in spite of certain death and suffering. Their joy is indomitable because they know that not even death can defeat it. They have nearly nothing in this world on which to base their joy, and so they are, at the same time, both *forced* and *blessed* to discover that **life's purest joy** is found in things that are **unending**.

If our response to suffering is rooted in the world, we will despair. But if our response to suffering is rooted in God's promises, we will rejoice always.

Uncertainty

Uncertainty, like suffering, also obscures our view of lasting joy by **surrounding us with the fog of fear and doubt**. How can we rejoice when the bills are well past due, the marriage on fragile ground, or the diagnosis or prognosis unknown?

It is difficult to rejoice when our **problems** threaten to eclipse our view of **the love of God**. When we allow ourselves to become overwhelmed with the uncertainties of life — the aches and pains of aging, the glum dark glass that is the future — our joy is placed in jeopardy. Just as fog reduces visibility, our sight of the source of true joy is obscured when we are not sure what is going to happen next.

The fog of uncertainty is more difficult to overcome than the barricade of sure suffering and death. Like the pre-dawn clouds, uncertainty offers momentary glimpses of true happiness and hope — before swooping in to obscure them again a moment later.

Spouses in a difficult relationship know the pain of uncertainty when, just as things seem to be getting better, the fighting resumes.

Parents of a child with a chronic or terminal condition also know the fog of uncertainty all too well.

Allow me to share another story of a *beautiful, strong* — and above all *joyful* — young woman named Emma.

Emma had cystic fibrosis, just like my son James.

Emma and James became hospital buddies over the years they spent as patients on the 2nd floor of Children's Hospital. They were not allowed to be in close contact for fear of cross-infection, but they enjoyed occasional games of "kickerball" in the courtyard along with games of *Battleship* during screen time visits from across the hospital.

Over time, it became apparent that Emma's case was more severe than my son's. She was eventually in the hospital nearly all the time. Specialists were unable to treat her as effectively as they had hoped, so Emma missed out on many childhood joys.

Researchers and doctors, that we knew and trusted, promised that a medication might be coming soon, which offered us a guarded measure of hope. But, as the months turned into years, our hope diminished as the thickening fog of uncertainty settled in.

Yet, somehow, Emma remained steadfastly *joyful* to the end.

At her funeral service, her youth pastor read 15-year-old Emma's Statement of Faith. She had been unable to participate fully in her Lutheran confirmation class because of her many hospitalizations, but she completed the curriculum before she passed from this life to the next — Emma's faith in Jesus was supremely important to her.

In spite of the fog of uncertainty that shrouded each day, Emma *knew* that God is not only real, but that *He loves us.* In her Statement of Faith, she declared that God's love, although sometimes hard to see, was not going to be diminished by the fog of her circumstances. She confessed her uncertainty about the near-term future but stood firm in her absolute certainty that God is love.

Her Statement of Faith was the most beautiful ode to joy that I had ever heard.

As the immense funeral crowd gathered that day to hear Emma's final epistle, we came to understand why this young, vibrant girl could smile so brightly while facing such grave challenges; she saw through the haze of uncertainty and chose to gaze upon the face of God. She refused to let uncertainty stand in her way.

Her joy was more than infectious — it was *invincible.* Her joy was not fleeting — it was sacred. Emma's joy was, in a word, *holy*.

Emma's witness still reminds me that we can rejoice in times of uncertainty and doubt — not because we are ignorant of life's terrible struggles but because we know what lies beyond the fog.

If our response to *uncertainty* is rooted in the world, we will despair. But if our response to uncertainty is rooted in *God's promises*, we will rejoice always.

False Joys

Finally, and perhaps most importantly, *false joys* are the greatest nemeses to *holy joy*.

Like a prison constructed of a million colorful balloons, the pleasures of this life entice us to stop our search for lasting happiness by offering us bouquets of immediate yet *temporary* glee.

Whether it is money, power, health, beauty or any other source of fleeting happiness the world has to offer, we are easily distracted in our search for *holy joy* by sirens, enticing us to indulge ourselves in the fleeting pleasure of *false joys*.

A final illustration:

One warm summer night, little James and I laid on our backs, looking at the stars on the patio of his 2nd floor hospital room. Like countless other parents throughout the ages, I pointed out traditional constellations to my son, like the Big Dipper and Cygnus the Swan, along with a few of our own that we called "Taun Taun" and "Star Destroyer."

As we looked to the sky, I felt a chill when I realized that just above us was the room where Jay had found perfect joy nearly a decade earlier.

Heaviness began to swell in my heart, and an old sorrow attempted to seep back in.

Then I remembered that old stargazer Abraham — how one of those countless stars God had shown him in Genesis 15 had been lit for Jay. And one for Emma. And one for James. And one for me.

We were part of a bigger story. Redemption's long song far outweighed my present lament. I was learning to see the source of holy joy even through the clouds of suffering and uncertainty.

But the greatest challenge to "rejoicing always" lay ahead.

A few years later, James' lungs were heading in the same direction that Emma's had. At his last check-up as a 15-year-old, we looked at a chart displaying a sobering, downward trend. Within a few short years, in spite of everyone's immense efforts, his lungs would almost certainly give out.

Then a miracle happened.

On James' 16th birthday, the new medication that James, Emma and the entire CF community had been hoping for was approved by the FDA. A month later, he started taking it. A week after that, his lungs were performing better than they had in a decade. Over time we came to see that this was no mere fluke — James' journey was now going to be a long one! The *heart wrenching uncertainty* of a terminal prognosis had given way to a new set of *happy uncertainties* — growing up, moving out, and — Lord willing — growing old!

It was nothing less than a miracle.

Our joy at this sudden change in James' health turned our entire family's outlook on its head. Even though this new medication was not *quite* a cure — we all began a new life.

But now, as months with this new medication have turned into years, I realize that, in some ways, my happy son is now facing a different set of obstacles to true joy — the obstacles of false joy that we all face when life is going well.

James is now able to enjoy a full slate of everything the world has to offer a brilliant and handsome young man — college, career, romance, etc. Yet I've come to recognize that even these pleasures — as wonderful as they can be — are not capable of producing joy that really lasts.

Adrift in a sea of colorful balloons, we are often distracted from the love of God by the temporary joys this world has to offer. Lasting happiness is traded for quick fixes. Pure joy is conceded for shabby substitutes. Even awful sin offers immense pleasure ... *but only for a season. (Hebrews 11:25)*

These false joys are the subject of the bulk of this book. Not because *suffering* and *uncertainty* aren't formidable joy-killers — *they are* — but because, for most of us, *the greatest threat to holy joy* is not the *brutal barrier of suffering* or even the *fearsome fog of uncertainty* but *the debilitating distraction of temporary pleasure.*

False joys cannot stand the test of time. We would be wise not to put too much stock in them. In the essays that follow, I will explore false joys — some obvious, some less so.

Less Real, Not Unreal

I realize, of course, that I sound like a killjoy.

That is not my intent.

When I speak of holy joy, I don't mean to carelessly write-off the blessings of the temporary joys we experience in life.

For example, *I enjoy balloons* — I even make balloon animals from time to time!

I also enjoy butterflies, old photographs, and memories.

Let me be perfectly clear: in the pages to follow, when I compare, what I call, false, temporary joys to holy joy, *I am not necessarily saying that those "false" joys are "bad."* In fact, they can be tremendous blessings! In the right context, and when received with thanksgiving, God blesses many of the earthly joys we experience. There is nothing inherently wrong with enjoying health, strength, wisdom, or wealth. I believe **God experiences joy when we rejoice in His blessings**.

Those temporary joys are unquestionably real.

What I am saying is that **holy joy** is even **more real**.

I considered using the word "lesser" instead of "false," but ultimately opted for the word "false." For one, it is more forceful. For another, some of the "false joys" that follow are more sinister than the word "lesser" implies.

So, please do not misunderstand my intent. I am not qualified to judge false joys ruthlessly. My aim is simply to **contrast** false joy with **holy joy** and, in so doing, illuminate holy joy more clearly.

It takes great faith to rejoice under the stars when they are hidden behind clouds. This is the type of joy that only the Holy Spirit can produce. It is a marvelous mystery!

May we always experience the wonder of holy joy as we draw and shed living water from the deepest well, the love of God in Christ Jesus.

For Discussion:
Who is one of the happiest people you know – and what struggles have they had to face in life?
Why are some people happy even when their circumstances are difficult – or even hopeless?
What is God saying to you about your happiness?

CHAPTER TWO:

REJOICE WHEN?

"Rejoice in the Lord always; again I will say, rejoice." (Philippians 4:4)

What is Paul talking about? Is he insane? Is he off his rocker? Does he have any clue what real life is like? Rejoice always?

What about when I'm depressed?

Rejoice, says Paul.

What about when I've completely blown it?

Rejoice then too. In fact, that's an excellent time to rejoice.

What about when I've made a fool of myself?

Double down. Rejoice away.

What about when failure is certain?

Oh yeah, says Paul. **Especially** *then. Rejoice like you have nothing to lose.*

It becomes disturbingly clear when we start to apply this teaching — *"Rejoice always"* — that joy is meant to transcend our present, temporary realities with an even bigger, eternal reality.

In other words, real joy doesn't have anything to do with being happy or sad, a success or failure, in chains or walking free. Real joy aims past our momentary troubles — as well as our momentary victories — and simply overrules all earthly sorrow (*and all earthly happiness too!*) with the invincible substance of **sacred joy** — something with more staying power.

As Paul writes (*while in chains!*) about this joy he's discovered in the love of God, his relationship with God runs miles deeper than any dungeon, stretches wider than any storm-ravaged sea, and reaches infinitely higher than we can imagine, even into the third Heaven, the place where God himself dwells.

How Can He Say That?

We might be tempted to write Paul off as a lunatic. Certainly, other people did before they got to know him. But when Paul says, "Rejoice *always*", even when we're suffering, even when the going is beyond rough... "rejoice *always*" — even when life is killing us — he has the chops to back it up.

He was no stranger to suffering. As a matter of fact, suffering for Christ is one of the defining characteristics of Paul's ministry.

He was jailed — many times.

He was beaten.

He was whipped.

Stripped naked.

Lost at sea.

You name it. If it was terrifying, awful, bad, painful, degrading, embarrassing, discouraging, depressing — Paul knew it firsthand.

If anyone had an excuse to say something different about joy, it was Paul. We would have understood if, instead of *"Rejoice always,"* Paul said something like,

"Rejoice later."

Or, *"Rejoice when you feel like it."*

Or, *"Rejoice after you get out of jail."*

Or, *"Rejoice after this storm blows over."*

Or, *"Rejoice when your heart's finally in it."*

No way, baby.

None of those things we might feel more comfortable hearing even register with Paul. Instead of saying something agreeable and comforting, he makes a madman's proclamation — "Rejoice *always*."

In other words, "Rejoice *all the time!*"

Be the "7-11" of joy. Joy doesn't close its doors for a little thing, like a pandemic. There's no vacation from joy, no day off, no off-day. Rejoice when your day crumbles. Rejoice when you lose your job. Rejoice when you are exposed as a fraud. Rejoice when you feel powerless to change the hell your life has become.

Rejoice when your life falls apart.

Yes, yes, yes! **That's exactly right!** says Paul. *Rejoice* **then**. Right *then — rejoice* **always!**

The Power to Rejoice

Ok, Paul has credibility. Most of us can acknowledge that. But ***how can you ask us to rejoice always?*** How can we rejoice when we are facing demons from our past that keep dragging us down? How can we rejoice when we've lived lives that bring us shame every time we think about that time when ... ? How can we rejoice when we've dug a hole of regret so deep and self-serving that there just doesn't seem to be any way out?

The power to rejoice in good times and bad simply cannot be faked. Any sort of hogwash, "I'm ok, you're ok" philosophy is so dishonest that it is powerless to produce lasting joy in the face of real shame and suffering. You and I simply don't have the imagination it takes to sustain a make-believe, pretend joy that is high enough, wide enough, and deep enough to lift us out of the miry pain that life presents us with almost every day.

False Joys: Only A Measure of Pleasure

Of course, we can temporarily fake joy by temporarily amusing ourselves. We could chase after any combination of ten thousand false joys, like health, wealth, wisdom, alcohol, drugs, social media, attention seeking *(is there any difference between social media and attention seeking?)*, philosophy, beauty, fame, and all manner of sin. These powerful distractions all bring a measure of pleasure — ***for a season***. They all offer relief from our brokenness, our self-pitying, our emptiness — but that relief is always — *and only* — temporary.

There's never enough alcohol. Never enough success. Never enough weight lost. Never enough muscle gained. The deeper our pain, the more voraciously we consume these false joys. The most deeply wounded among us always have the most outrageously oversized addictions.

The false joys of the flesh are all worthless — chasing after the wind — because none of those false joys last as long as we need them to, stretch as far as we need them to go, or cut as carefully and surgically as our painful past requires.

Therapists talk about "maladaptive coping mechanisms", which are behaviors and choices people make in response to trauma — big trauma, little trauma, or sustained micro-traumas. Either way, we all deal with different kinds of trauma eventually. For example, if a child is abandoned, they might try to cope with the pain and shame through drinking or drugs. It's an escape. It provides quick and fleeting relief, but the damage continues to spread slowly and steadily.

As anesthesia goes, it's hard to beat chemicals, and yet anesthesia doesn't have to be chemical in nature. It can manifest as an unreasonable drive for success or a quest to gain control by trying to look thinner and thinner. They're all false anesthetics, all the wrong prescription. All false joys.

When the anesthesia wears off, the wound still remains. The constant degradation of drunkenness doesn't heal anything — it just masks the pain for a short while. This is why addictions and obsessions tend to spiral out of control — they don't deal with the source of the fire raging inside us. They merely supply more fuel.

It's clear that we need something more substantive than the false joys the world has to offer if we're going to experience the holy joy that Paul is talking about here. We need a source of joy that is bigger than our imagination, more profound than our philosophy, and so utterly real that everything else seems like vapor.

In other words, we need God.

More specifically, we need to find our truest joy in the truest place: the holy, abiding, unchanging love of God. We need God to intervene and pull us out of the pit that we can't get out of either on our own or with the help of our friends.

We need God to overrule our guilt and shame in a way that reveals "positive thinking" as whitewash.

We need God to judge our sins and call them what they are — lame, shabby substitutes for real joy.

And we need God to do the impossible — to take away all our sin, remove all our shame, heal all our pain, and make us new again. We need, in every way, to be born again into a new kind of joy only available through the power of God.

Only God can do these things. And I know of no clearer demonstration of God's intervention in our suffering than the cross of Jesus Christ of Nazareth, the King of the Jews.

With human effort, redemption on the level we need is simply impossible. Therapy and medication are helpful tools, but they cannot redeem us. However, with God, all things are possible. Manmade joy is ultimately a fleeting shadow — temporary at best. But the joy that comes from being redeemed, being loved by God in spite of ourselves, from receiving our adoption as beloved sons and daughters of God overcomes any fear of abandonment. Any chains, any disappointment, any sorrow, any grief, and any storm that the world hurls our way mean nothing when compared with the ultimate joy of being our Abba's child.

God is greater than any wall we can construct around ourself, and His love for us is more real than anything we've ever experienced. That is the reason we have for joy, and why we can boldly stand our ground in any trial or tribulation. This joy that transcends our mundane human existence is holy because it comes from God.

This is the reason we can join with Paul in saying, "Rejoice *always*."

Abiding in Joy

Yet, the challenge remains: how do we follow through on this command to abide in holy joy **always**? There are three clues to sustaining and abiding in holy joy in those two words in Philippians 4:4 — "Rejoice always."

First Clue: Joy is a Choice

If you paid attention in school, you understand that the word "rejoice" is an imperative — in other words, it is a ***command***. That means it is an order to be obeyed by some sort of action.

And what is that action we are to choose?

Rejoicing often requires a shift in perspective. Like a photographer trying to capture the big picture, we have to zoom out, use the wide-angle lens of eternal perspective to see past our present circumstances and recapture a Heaven-sized perspective on our lives.

In other words, we get distracted from eternal joy by temporary things:

Suffering is like a *wall that blocks our view of holy joy.*

Uncertainty is like a *fog that brings us anxiety and hides holy joy from our eyes.*

And **false joys** are like *party balloons that distract our attention from holy joy.*

When our view of eternal joy is obstructed by walls of temporary suffering, the fog of uncertainty or the pretty balloons of false joys, we must recognize it and train ourselves to shift perspective — to zoom out, and hunt for the view from heaven.

Holy joy — "always-on" joy — is a deliberate choice to shift perspective.

Second Clue: Joy is a Group Activity

You might find it interesting to note, as I did only recently, that the command to rejoice is plural. In English it is hard to catch, but Paul is basically saying, "You — *all of you, together, in community* — choose joy."

There are times in my life when I've felt like I could make it on my own. But I was wrong. I still try to do things on my own now and then, but it usually doesn't take long for me to realize what a mistake that is. I don't know why I fall into that trap of thinking I don't need anyone else. But the truth is we all need each other. God designed us that way. We need each other for encouragement. We need each other for correction. We need each other for perspective.

Holy joy is ultimately a communal experience. If God Himself is a community held together by love (Father, Son, and Spirit all bound together by love), we must find joy in the context of a community where love is the glue. We are in this together. God ordained it to be that way. Nobody discovers lasting joy all by themselves. If we ever hope to rejoice always, we've got to do it in fellowship with one another.

Real joy cannot be fully experienced apart from community.

Third Clue (and Most Important): God's Joy is the Only Source of Everlasting Joy

I suppose I made my position clear earlier, but I need to say it again so there is no mistaking me for a peddler of positive thinking or a mere motivational speaker. I am called to preach the gospel — the best news — and for me the cross of Jesus Christ will always remain the only reason anyone could possibly rejoice *always.*

I would be negligent as a Bible teacher if I did not direct you to Paul's specific words in Philippians 4:4: "Rejoice *in the Lord* always." He drives it home again in the next verse, declaring that "*The Lord* is near." And in case you missed it the first two times, in the passage just after that, Paul affirms that all anxiety dissolves and is replaced with peace when we present our prayers and petitions with thanksgiving ... *to God.* God at the beginning, God at the end, God at the center.

Sometimes Christians forget that our God is the God of joy. We remember Him as the God who provides, protects, redeems, and restores — and those are all good. But Yahweh is also the God who *delights*, who *celebrates*, who *rejoices* in His children when we turn to Him.

> *"I know what it is to be in need,*
> *and I know what it is to have plenty.*
> *I have learned the secret of being content*
> *in any and every situation,*
> *whether well fed or hungry,*
> *whether living in plenty or in want.*

I can do all this through him
who gives me strength."
(Philippians 4:12-13)

Because our God is the God of joy, we are to be a people marked by unstoppable joy, whether we are in chains or free, well fed or hungry, living in plenty or want. We can rejoice always, not because we have the talent or skill to manufacture holy joy, but because God's joy has given us all the reason we need to walk together with all joy, always.

For Discussion:
Is joy more a choice or a feeling?
Is joy optional for a Christian?
Why would God command us to experience joy in the context of community?

CHAPTER THREE:
YOU DON'T KNOW WHAT YOU'VE GOT TILL IT'S GONE

When the Lord restored the fortunes of Zion,
we were like those who dream.
Then our mouth was filled with laughter,
and our tongue with shouts of joy;
then they said among the nations,
"The Lord has done great things for them."
The Lord has done great things for us;
we are glad.

Restore our fortunes, O Lord,
like streams in the Negeb!
Those who sow in tears
shall reap with shouts of joy!

He who goes out weeping,
bearing the seed for sowing,
shall come home with shouts of joy,
bringing his sheaves with him.
(Psalm 126)

If we are going to talk about joy, we have to deal with the inescapable issue of suffering. How can we "rejoice always" when suffering is an undeniable part of our daily lives?

You Don't Know What You've Got Till It's Gone

Joni Mitchell's song, *Big Yellow Taxi*, sums up the very real pain of loss in a way that resonates with many:

> *Don't it always seem to go*
> *That you don't know what you've got*
> *'Till it's gone*
> *They paved paradise*
> *And they put up a parking lot*
> *(Joni Mitchell, Big Yellow Taxi)*

Sadly, the joy of innocence is lost somewhere along the way for each of us. Paradise gets paved beneath the traffic of life. Asphalt keeps compounding on the poor choices we've made, and, in spite of our sincerity, we find that our best efforts to improve things somehow end up making them worse. From an all-too-early age, the paradise planted in each of our hearts by a loving God is subject to the regular resurfacing of heavy choices — and even heavier regrets.

As layer upon layer of life's dark asphalt is laid down over our innocence, we must ask: *who is driving the steamroller?* **Who is responsible** for paving our joy?

While it would be easy to join the world's chorus and blame others, or the hand we've been dealt, the only viable answer is **ourselves**.

There is no question that, even before we're born, the baggage of simply being human has already begun to pave the paradise and the joy we were designed to experience. The Bible has a very hard teaching that many stumble on — it is that we are all **born** into sin. And while this is an unappealing thought, it seems a reasonable description of what it means to be born into **any family**.

While we are still being knit together in the womb, our parents' past choices, family politics, and family secrets entangle us before we can take our first breath. Paradise was paved before we even got here. The sins of our fathers may not be our fault, but there is no denying that we inherit their consequences. And all too soon after our births, we contribute to this traffic and misery, a concept that the theologians describe as "original sin." While it is without question an unappealing and unhappy doctrine — *not all truth is welcome or pleasant* — anyone can see that it is true.

We can't blame our parents for our paved paradise for very long, though.

There comes a day when we climb into the seat of the steamroller and begin to work the controls for ourselves, paving what's left of the paradise in our hearts. Like Adam and Eve before us, the day comes for each of us when we pluck that fruit ... and we know, firsthand, the difference between good and evil. There is no turning back. Eventually, whatever innocence childhood brought us is lost as we make our own choices and lay new layers of pavement.

And with the loss of innocence, ***joy is also lost***.

Fig Leaves and Fancy Stitching

Maybe you prefer a Biblical example instead of me quoting Joni Mitchell. Do you remember the first thing Adam and Eve did when they realized they were naked in Genesis Chapter 3? They tried to cover up! They sewed fig leaves together to conceal themselves. They paved paradise — *or at least put a robe on it*.

Lest we think we're any better than they were, we all do exactly the same thing when we are caught in our sin. We try to plaster over our poor choices with even poorer excuses. Some of us try to cover the past with lies. Some of us perform good deeds. Some of us become religious. It does not matter what pavement, plaster, or papier mache we choose — there is no covering made by human hands that can restore our innocence.

The false joys we bronze our brokenness with are fig leaves, golden calves, false gods. Feeding our egos, seeking pleasure, indulging in escapism, religion, or accomplishments ... all of them seem like good ideas at first. While some of our coping mechanisms may be appropriate in measured use, none of the false joys we chase are adequate to restore our deepest spiritual fortunes and, therefore, cannot recover our greatest joy. The stitchings we might cobble together are simply insufficient to cover our nakedness and shame.

If the story ended with Adam and Eve's cheap costumes, we would have no hope at all. But joy can be restored from our tears, and our nakedness can be covered in stunning, celestial robes. While we can't restore paradise, God can. It is the Lord who restores joy and the fortunes of Zion, not us. Fig leaves crumble and fall apart; what we need is a new robe tailored by Heaven's haberdasher — the Lord Jesus Christ.

> *"For in this tent we groan,*
> *longing to put on our heavenly dwelling,*
> *if indeed by putting it on we may not be found naked.*
> *For while we are still in this tent, we groan, being burdened*
> *— not that we would be unclothed,*
> *but that we would be further clothed,*
> *so that what is mortal may be swallowed up by life.*
> *He who has prepared us for this very thing is God,*
> *who has given us the Spirit as a guarantee."*
> *(2 Corinthians 5:1-5)*

For those of us who believe, Jesus is the lamb who was slain and tanned. We no longer turn to fig leaves and false joys to hide our shame. We wear a new robe made of pure lambskin.

After dying on the cross, Jesus was raised from the dead, and He re-opened paradise for good. With a mighty hand and an outstretched arm, He tore through the dismal asphalt of our sin, removing layered cakes of tar and brimstone to uncover paradise, restore our fortunes, and bring us true joy. All we need to do is invite Him into the jobsite of our hearts — and give Him plenty of room to work. Have we invited Him yet? His hand is the only one that can save us. His sacrifice on the cross is our salvation, the only way to experience the joy we've been looking for.

Tears Like Seeds

We've been talking about holy joy — *real* joy, *true* joy, *lasting* joy. Not the paper-thin, fleeting joy that we can patch together for a little while by entertaining ourselves. We've been investigating the joy that is incorruptible and infallible, the kind that only God can bring us.

I've searched the Scriptures for references to joy and discovered an astonishing pattern: *the greatest times of joy* in the scriptures *come after the times of deepest suffering*.

Joy is nearly always a second experience, usually coming after significant loss, pain, or suffering. "Joy comes in the morning," (Psalm 30:5) — *but only after a night of bitter anguish.* The children of Israel rejoiced greatly when the temple was restored — *after it had been destroyed due to their negligence.* The widow rejoiced when she found her coin — *but only after it had been lost.* The father rejoiced when the prodigal came home — *but only after he resigned himself to the fact that his son may have been lost forever.*

It is almost as though suffering and pain are the seeds of joy.

Not surprisingly, that is exactly what Psalm 126 says:

> *"He who goes out weeping,*
> *bearing the seed for sowing,*
> *shall come home with shouts of joy,*
> *bringing his sheaves with him."*
> *(Psalm 126:6)*

When you think about it, this verse makes perfect sense — just as we don't know what we've got till it's gone, we don't appreciate something until after it has been lost. Loss makes us appreciate even more the people and things we have left.

We don't appreciate being full until we've been hungry. We don't appreciate health until we've been sick. We don't appreciate being found until we've been lost. We don't know the joy of salvation if we haven't first experienced the havoc of sin.

We don't truly appreciate the lofty mountain's grandeur until we've walked through the shadows in the valley. We don't truly appreciate the truth until we've lived a lie. We don't truly appreciate peace until we've known war, security until we've faced danger, prosperity until we have known poverty.

"Those who sow in tears shall reap with shouts of joy!"
(Psalm 126:5)

If tears are the seeds of joy, I would like to share with you three observations about the harvest — the sheaves of joy — those seeds of suffering produce.

Suffering Produces the Joyful Sheaves of Sight

In other words, when we experience the sorrow of loss, we gain perspective on what matters most. Ask anyone who has received a terminal or chronic medical diagnosis. Suddenly, life's priorities snap into perspective. Trivial matters that used to cause worry and stress simply become unimportant, and what truly matters is illuminated. Eternal and significant things, like faith, family, friends, and relationships, come into focus while temporary and insignificant things, like money, material items, or prestige, fade into obscurity. Suffering is a seed that brings the joy of clear sight.

Suffering Fuels the Joyful Sheaves of Service

When we go through suffering, we develop compassion for those who also suffer, and this fuels the tremendous joy of serving others. I have received countless meals at our San Diego Ronald McDonald House over the years as a parent of a hospitalized child. Different businesses, churches, and community groups generously serve the meals there each day. Yet some of my fondest memories are of those times when the volunteers serving the meals were friends and families of children who were once inpatient themselves.

One time, a Polynesian family of a child who had been very

ill (and thankfully recovered) put on a full luau for the families at the Ronald McDonald House, complete with live music and hula dancing! Emma's family also prepared a meal one December evening after she passed.

Those who have suffered are inspired to serve those enduring similar trials. Cancer survivors often volunteer at the cancer clinic, people who have formerly experienced homelessness often volunteer at soup kitchens. When we have been through the valley of the shadow of death, we find ourselves drawn to serve those going through it now — there is great joy to be found in serving someone in need, just as we were served when we needed it. Suffering is a seed that catalyzes service.

Suffering Stirs the Joyful Sheaves of Saving

Finally, any of us who have been set free find it impossible to remain unmoved by the crushing burdens of those around us. We feel an urgency to help others detour from the broad pavement leading to destruction and follow the narrow path to paradise. We know that we can bring our tears to Jesus and watch Him turn them to joy — and that compels us to share the good news with others in need.

The angels know it, and we who believe know it too — there is no greater cause for joy and celebration than when one who is lost comes home to the Lord, and paradise is restored in their hearts. Suffering is a seed that may bloom into salvation.

Joy Fully Restored

As good as it can get here on earth after our heart's parking lot has been broken up and paradise has been restored through Jesus Christ, we know that the story is not over.

We will still encounter times of sorrow and tears. On this side of glory, even when we have abandoned our own steamrollers and sins, someone around us is probably just getting theirs warmed up.

While we await the Lord's return, there will be someone trying to pave the paradise regained in us. But we don't have to let them get us down because we have a hope higher than the heavens are above the earth.

Tears and sorrow will not go away until every knee bows and Jesus comes back to make everything new. But we do have this promise: there won't be tears in Heaven. Praise God! We look forward to that wondrous day when this old, groaning parking lot will be scraped clean forever and a new heaven, a new earth — and a new paradise — firmly established.

> *"When the Lord restored the fortunes of Zion,*
> *we were like those who dream.*
> *Then our mouth was filled with laughter,*
> *and our tongue with shouts of joy;"*
> *(Psalm 126:1-2a)*

Lord, restore the fortunes of all your children.
Lord, restore unto us your everlasting joy.
Lord, haste the day!

For Discussion:
Who is most responsible for our suffering: ourselves, others, or causes beyond our control?
What role does forgiveness play in finding true happiness?
What is God saying to you about turning your suffering into an opportunity to serve others?

CHAPTER FOUR:
THE FALSE JOY OF KEEPING SCORE

"Love keeps no record of wrongs."
(1 Corinthians 13:5b, NIV)

Recently, Bob and Betty, my father- and mother-in-law, celebrated their 50th wedding anniversary. Our kids were with us as we celebrated, so I thought it would be a wonderful opportunity to ask them for the secret to reaching 50 years of marriage.

They both said the same thing: "Don't keep score."

Roy, Bob's father, said the exact same thing to Tammie and me at our wedding. He and Bob's mother were joyfully married for more than 69 years.

There must be something to it!

When life disappoints us — when we're wounded and hurt by others — we are all tempted to pursue the false joy of keeping score. But keeping a record of wrongs committed against us by others is a joyless, dead-end road. It may feel good to blame others for a time, but in the end, such pettiness drains all of the joy out of a relationship.

Like Scrooge accounting for every debt owed to him, our hearts shrivel into a splinter of coal when we cling to keeping a record of the wrongs done to us. Victimhood is a dark anchor in the heart.

Joy Lost: "You Owe Me"

The root of the problem is the sin of **blame**.

Our society has turned blaming others into a highly ritualized, quasi-civil right.

If I get in a car accident, even if I clearly caused it, I am encouraged to blame the other driver. If a child causes trouble at school, parents rush to blame the teacher or other students. How many educators have heard the words, "My child would never do that," even when everyone saw them do it?

If my life falls apart because of the irresponsible, reckless, and foolish choices I've made, who do I blame? My parents. My upbringing. My childhood environment — everything and everyone *but myself.*

Nothing breeds bitterness quite so well as those words — *"it's your fault."*

Joy Restored: "I Owe You"

When we fall into the devil's trap of thinking we are owed *anything* by anyone else, we are setting ourselves up for bitterness, stunted spiritual development, and downright joyless living. Holy joy is attainable only after we take this truth to heart: *no one owes me anything.*

To grow beyond the joyless modes of self-pity and score-keeping, we must first take responsibility for ourselves. We are not owed a living. We are not guaranteed a fair shake. The world is under no obligation to make our lives fun, easy, or painless.

Only after we set sail on that heading can we finally move past lingering over the wreckage of unchangeable yesterdays and discover the greatest joy.

And that joy comes into focus when we realize that happiness is never found in blaming others — *but in blessing them instead.* Instead of demanding that we get what we want from others, we surrender our "rights" and bless those who harm us, give to those who take from us, and love those who hate us.

This is, admittedly, the black belt of discipleship — to actually hear and do the words of Jesus, who calls us to bless those who curse us. Fortunately, He showed us that it is possible to forgive those who harm us when He prayed for His killers on the cross: "Forgive them, for they know not what they do."

Does Jesus keep score against those who crucified Him? Just the opposite. He has the guts to bless even the haters who hammer Him to a wooden post. There is no scorekeeping here; no record of wrongs tucked away somewhere. With His words from the cross, Jesus tore up and threw away the score sheet. Love incarnate, He kept no record of their wrongs.

My good friend Alan Johnson once shared some expert scorekeeping advice: "Give up all hope of a better past."

We find real joy in forgiving and blessing those who have wronged us, not in keeping records of wrongs. The weight of our ledgers filled with journal entries of blaming others holds us back from maturity. The chains of the past are broken only after we forgive courageously, just as our master taught us to do — and did Himself.

The sooner we can get past the petulant demands of believing we are owed anything by anyone else, the sooner we can get on to the adult work of taking responsibility for our lives, leaving behind the joyless track of blaming and judging others.

"Owe no one anything, except to love each other, for the one who loves another has fulfilled the law." (Romans 13:8)

I'd like to share three score cards we should never keep.

Scorecards Against Others

"Judge not, and you will not be judged; condemn not, and you will not be condemned; forgive, and you will be forgiven; give, and it will be given to you. Good measure, pressed down, shaken together, running over, will be put into your lap. For with the measure you use it will be measured back to you." (Luke 6:37-38)

Do you remember the Lord's prayer? I'm specifically thinking about the part where Jesus says, "Forgive us our trespasses as we forgive those who trespass against us." There is an expectation in that this prayer that the way God forgives us is the way we should forgive others.

Jesus warned: "Don't judge others," and "With the measure you use, it will be measured to you." In other words, in the same way we forgive others their wrongs, He will forgive our wrongs. When we pray, "forgive us our trespasses", we are saying to God,

"The same way I forgive others is how I want you to forgive me. If I'm stingy, be stingy with me. If I'm generous, be generous with me. If I keep score and blame others, then Lord, do the same to me."

Charles Spurgen said that if we don't forgive others, we sign our own death warrant every time we say the Lord's prayer.

Do we want to experience the joy of being forgiven by God? Then we must forgive those who have wronged us, not keep a scorecard against others. We must stop blaming others for our unhappiness.

Only then can we experience the fullness of God's forgiveness and truly know the joy of being set free from the heavy millstone of judgment.

The Scorecard Against Ourselves

While most people are experts at blaming others, for some of us, the hardest person to forgive is ourselves. We know very well that some of our greatest life's tragedies are our own fault. Whether by sins of commission or omission, our lives took a turn for the worse, and regret haunts us each day as we consider what might have been. We languish in dungeons of the past, which we cannot change.

When we find ourselves in this place, the Holy Spirit has a message we need to hear:

"There is therefore now no condemnation
for those who are in Christ Jesus."
(Romans 8:1)

That doesn't mean we didn't do anything wrong, as some people mistakenly interpret it. It means that, in Jesus Christ and through His atoning death and life-giving resurrection from the dead, we have been forgiven for every wrong we have ever done.

"No condemnation" is hardly worth mentioning for someone who doesn't deserve condemnation. But for the rest of us — the scoundrels and scalawags, the ragamuffins and real sinners among us — the offer of no condemnation in Christ Jesus is precious. "No condemnation" means something only for those who know that we deserve full condemnation.

If a man pulls another man out of a pit, we call that a rescue; it is salvation. But if that man never fell into a pit in the first place, he doesn't need to be rescued. We have all fallen into a ditch. If it isn't obvious just by looking around, the Bible makes it clear when it says, *"For all have sinned and fall short of the glory of God." (Romans 3:23)*

Ultimately, the scores we've got are the scores we've earned. We have, each one of us, made choices of our volition worthy of condemnation. Mercy and grace must start from that position of understanding, or they have no meaning at all. If I don't come to Jesus as a sinner, Jesus can do nothing for me. If I do not come as a sinner, I don't need the cross.

The world today thinks it doesn't need Jesus because it is so busy blaming others that it is completely blind to its own sin.

Now, I recognize that I have just painted a very bleak picture of the world. But thank God, that is not where the story ends. In fact, recognizing our brokenness is where the story truly begins.

The Scriptures say this about the promise of Christ to wipe clean our spiritual scorecard:

If we confess our sins, he is faithful and just and will forgive us our sins and purify us from all unrighteousness. (1 John 1:9)

No condemnation. No record of wrongs to keep against ourselves. The freedom to move on, to start fresh, to be set free from the breakdowns of the past.

If God has trashed our scorecard, then who are we to keep it?

A Scorecard Against God

"Who is this that darkens counsel by words without knowledge?" (Job 38:2)

Finally, we have to address the reality that we are all, from time to time, tempted to blame God for our troubles. The truth is that God, Himself, sometimes leads us into trials and testing. And, if we are honest about our feelings, those trials may seem pointless and downright unfair.

When God leads us through trials, He never does it so without a reason; it is always redemptive. Every challenge God leads us through is an opportunity to teach us new things or bless others as we simply remain faithful to Him and trust that He is at work — even in the hard times. More importantly, God never leaves us to walk through our trials alone. His Holy Spirit is always there — at every uphill step — to comfort, to cheer, and to guide.

No one serves as a better example of someone who could have blamed God for his hard life than Joseph.

You may remember the epic Bible story — as a young boy, God gave dreams to Joseph, showing him that he would one day bring deliverance to his extensive family. As his life went on, however, things went from bad to worse for Joseph. He was sold into slavery by his brothers then sent to die in prison in a foreign country even though he committed no crime.

If anyone had a reason to blame God for the pain in his life, it was Joseph. But Joseph held firm in his faith that God was ultimately good and that God was in control. Joseph believed that even the horrific trials he was going through were part of a bigger plan for good.

Years later, because he never lost faith in God, Joseph became second in charge under Pharaoh. When a famine threatened to wipe out his family far away, Joseph was able to not only rescue them all, but to provide his brothers and his father with blessing upon blessing.

But there comes a pivotal moment in Joseph's story when he finally has the opportunity for revenge — to blame his brothers, drag out the scorecard and remind them of their evil sin of selling him into slavery. At that time, Joseph also had the opportunity to *blame God* for making his life so hard. But do you remember what Joseph said to his brothers?

"As for you, you meant evil against me,
but God meant it for good,
to bring it about that many people
should be kept alive, as they are today."
(Genesis 50:20)

In the face of overwhelming trials, Joseph trusted that God was at work in all of it. Rather than blaming God for his situation, Joseph chose to respond in faith to God's guidance.

Joseph wasn't the only one who refused to keep score and curse God for his troubles. There was also Job, who suffered dearly at God's hand but still held on to his faith that God was in control. I could go on to mention David, Jeremiah, Isaiah, Paul, Peter, James, and John, and many personal friends who could have blamed God for the difficult things that happened to them, yet ultimately chose, instead, to see that God was at work in their lives, and that He was working all things together for good.

And in spite of their trials, they found joy.

Let us tear up the scorecards we keep against others, against ourselves, and against God. Let's kick the self-destructive habit of passing around blame for a past we cannot change.

Instead, let's look forward to a new day, a new start, a new life made complete in the holy joy of forgiveness.

For Discussion:
Have you ever been "unforgiven" by someone? How does it feel?
Who have you found yourself keeping score against?
Is it ever appropriate to keep score?

Chapter Five:
The False Joy of Looking Back

*"Not that I have already obtained this or am already perfect,
but I press on to make it my own, because Christ Jesus has
made me his own. Brothers, I do not consider that I have made
it my own. But one thing I do: forgetting what lies behind and
straining forward to what lies ahead, I press on toward the goal
for the prize of the upward call of God in Christ Jesus."*
(Philippians 3:12-14)

*"Is not this what we said to you in Egypt:
'Leave us alone that we may serve the Egyptians'?
For it would have been better for us to serve the
Egyptians than to die in the wilderness."*
*"The Lord said to Moses, 'Why do you cry to me?
Tell the people of Israel to go forward.'"*
(Exodus 14:12,15)

Joy Lost: Dwelling on the Past

A friend recently saw a photo displayed in my living room of my wife and me on our wedding day. "Wow," he exclaimed, looking back and forth between me and the photo, genuinely shocked. "You've changed!"

I had hair then and was definitely ... **smaller.**

If I spend too much time looking at that snapshot from the past, it would be easy to join Paul McCartney, singing, *"Yesterday, all my troubles seemed so far away."*

But were the "old days" really so **good?** I may have been younger, thinner and better looking, but I was also more impulsive, more foolish, and always broke!

Yesterday is never really as glamorous as pop music makes it out to be. While we all tend to romanticize the past, it wasn't really the way the Carpenters memorialized it in the song, "*Yesterday Once More*," or even the way Archie Bunker and Edith made it sound when they sang "*Those Were the Days.*"

Most of us are looking for joy by **straining backward** instead of **straining ahead**. But looking back in life doesn't produce lasting joy. Like the children of Israel, who experienced the burden of freedom as they left slavery in Egypt, we tend to gloss over the bad aspects of the past. When the going gets tough, we long for the strangely comforting feel of our old chains.

Looking back may be comforting, but in the end, it is a false joy — it never brings true happiness.

God says to each one of us today what He said to the children of Israel back then: "Go forward." (Exodus 14:15b). The land of promise lies ahead, not behind us. We will only experience true joy — the land of milk and honey — by straining ahead, by pressing forward, toward the joy of the goal God has set before us.

Mythed Opportunities

Have you ever seen pressed flowers? They are beautiful, **but they are also dead**. Pressed flowers, although pleasant to look at, are little more than memories fixed in time. A pressed flower has no hope, no future. We easily forfeit our hope and our future — **our joy** — by allowing ourselves to become stuck in a moment, enchanted by the pressed flowers from our past.

A myth distorts the past in order to enshrine an oversimplified view of reality. When we are enamored with yesterday, we tend to distort its truth, glossing over the bad parts. We over-romanticize the things we liked. And so, we convince ourselves to believe in a myth — **the myth of the good old days**.

If we could set aside the rose-colored lenses through which

we view the past, we would very likely come to realize the painful truth that the past was *never quite as happy as we remember it*. We must always work to keep the past in perspective in order to avoid mythologizing it.

If I choose to live looking backward, I become a pressed flower — stagnant, unable to grow or experience wonder and joy at each new day's revelation of God and His creation.

I must make a disclaimer here: remembering the past — especially what God has done for us — can often be helpful. I'm not saying we should not remember the past **at all** – only that we should remember it **soberly** and **accurately**, being careful to learn from it without mythologizing it. As one of my all-time favorite Christian music groups, Petra, put it:

> *"Sometimes it's good to look back down,*
> *We've come so far - we've gained such ground*
> *But joy is not in where we've been,*
> *Joy is who's waiting at the end"*
> *(Road to Zion, words by Mike Hudson)*

A good past is often the enemy of the best future. Whatever **good** there may have been in "the good ole days" is **nothing** compared to the glory that God is revealing in us each new day — and the glory He will reveal on the Last Day. We are not called to gaze backward down the trail but to press forward and follow Him to greater heights.

For a genuine follower of Jesus, we find deep joy in knowing that our best days are always ahead. If we live to recapture the mythical good days of the past, we will miss the very best that God has prepared for us today.

Divine Discontent

We are talking here about divine discontentment. Of course, the Scriptures teach us to be content with **what we have**, but we must never be content with **who we are**. Who I was yesterday and who I am today must never become more important than who I am straining to become in Christ.

If we wish to find true joy in life, we must never be content with who we are right now. We must wake ourselves up from the easy slumber of self-satisfaction; put an end to snoozing our days away in spiritual complacency. True joy is found when we are **divinely unsettled**, filled with wonder, and ready to learn new things from God.

"Forget the former things; do not dwell on the past.
See, I am doing a new thing!
Now it springs up; do you not perceive it?
I am making a way in the wilderness
and streams in the wasteland."
(Isaiah 43:18-19)

Growth Heartset

*"...forgetting what lies behind and **straining forward** to what lies ahead, I press on..." (Philippians 3:13b)*

In Philippians 3, even the great apostle Paul says that he does not consider himself an expert but a mere novice in the ways of Christ. He claims he has not yet arrived. Yes, Paul most certainly believed in the kingdom come, when all the colors would bleed into one. We know Paul believed it — **but he was still running**.

Paul clearly trusted that Jesus broke the bonds and loosed the chains, carried the cross and alli his shame — but Paul also knew he had **further to go**. He confessed that he had "not yet attained all this" or been made perfect. Paul still hadn't found what he was looking for — complete surrender to the will of God.

Educators know the importance of having a "growth mind-set."

Someone with a growth mindset is open to new things and can be taught, whereas someone who has a settled mindset is unteachable. I would make an important distinction in applying this principle to our spiritual life. While education is specifically concerned with transforming our **minds**, discipleship is focused on transforming our **entire lives**.

Therefore, true joy, in the life of a follower of Jesus Christ, requires more than a mere growth **mindset**, rather a growth **heartset** because the heart is the source from which all behavior, life, and attitude flows.

Discipleship may rightfully include intellectual elements, but it is much bigger than that. Full discipleship transcends academic growth and seeks to reform our very hearts, renovate our deepest character, and strengthen our daily walk. In that sense, discipleship is more **socialization** than **education** — more a matter of refining the whole life than merely the development of gray matter.

A great athlete must be coachable. A truly great person must be teachable. If we want to become irrelevant and lose our edge, all we need to do is become **complacent**. But if we want to excel in whatever we do, we must learn to **never be satisfied with the victories of the past**.

Holy joy is not found by lingering in the rear-view mirror. Since all false joys are temporary — ultimately fading into the past — seeking these types of joy is essentially the same as straining to look to the past. Holy joy beckons us to strain toward the horizon ahead. The joy of the kingdom of Heaven belongs to those who become like children and acknowledge that there is much more to learn as we follow Jesus.

No matter how settled we are on certain issues, there is always a reason to be **unsettled**, to grow, learn, sharpen the image even more, and redraw the kingdom in our hearts with precision each day.

Here are three keys to recovering a growth heartset — and, therefore, learning true joy.

Be Teachable

"Make me to know your ways, O Lord;
teach me your paths."
(Psalm 25:4)

To keep growing, we must remain teachable. We must never assume we have arrived at a full understanding of **anything**. No matter how much we have learned, there is always more to discover. No matter how smart we feel, God is smarter. We must be open-minded, not in the sense of embracing every opinion as fact, but in the sense of testing every idea for truth, discarding the portions that aren't. Being open-minded is not the same as being tender-minded. In fact, I have discovered that an open mind is generally a *tougher mind*!

> *"I am sending you out like sheep among wolves.*
> *Therefore be as shrewd as snakes and as innocent as doves."*
> *(Matthew 10:16)*

A believer should not be afraid to occasionally read books or listen to radio and opinions that disagree with us — not to slothfully absorb these opposing ideas but to vigorously thresh the truth from the chaff. Exercising with an opponent makes us stronger and wiser. Remember, whatever we learned yesterday is not the end of knowledge. There is always more to learn today.

Be Reachable

> *"As it is said, 'Today, if you hear his voice,*
> *do not harden your hearts as in the rebellion.'"*
> *(Hebrews 3:15)*

To discover the joy of a growth heartset, we must also be **reachable**. Restoring joy by establishing a growth heartset requires that we be willing **to hear God's voice**. Sometimes His voice is like thunder, sometimes it's a whisper. If we aren't listening for Him to speak, we will never hear Him. We must be careful not to so overload our schedules with urgent tasks that we forget the most important job of all: to be available to answer God when He calls each day.

We must make it a discipline and steady practice to set aside a daily time to hear from God. This should include time spent studying the Scriptures, praying for one another and ourselves, and simply quieting our minds so that we can hear from Him.

In addition to these essential methods for being reachable to God, there are dozens of others. God may speak to us through books, music, film, fellowship, worship, serving others, or even a hard conversation with our enemies! Regardless of our preferred mode of discovery, we must learn to approach the Lord with the doors of our hearts unbarred and our schedules open to whatever He might have.

Be Impeachable

Finally, I believe that to experience true joy by developing a growth heartset, we must also be *impeachable*.

Allow me to explain. To impeach someone is to cast doubt on them. And self-doubt is always where the greatest spiritual growth takes place. Let me be clear: I am not talking about doubting God, which is properly a different discipline altogether. I am talking about the healthy habit of honestly questioning ourselves. In other words, if we wish to develop a growth heartset, we must be eager to question our motives and our thoughts to *"see if there be any wicked way in me."* (Psalm 139:24)

To be impeachable means to be willing to subject our thoughts, our opinions, and our footsteps to the sobering practice of self-reflection. Thus, in order to grow into the holy joy of full discipleship, we must each be willing to cast doubt on our own understanding at times. It also means that we must judge ourselves with a more critical eye than anyone else.

A joy-filled Christian is not afraid of self-doubt because healthy self-doubt is the dock from which every meaningful self-discovery is launched.

"For by the grace given to me
I say to everyone among you
not to think of himself more highly than he ought to think,

but to think with sober judgment,
each according to the measure of faith
that God has assigned."
(Romans 12:3)

For Discussion:
What are the risks of "straining backward" – dwelling on the past?
Are your best days behind you or ahead?
How can you work on developing a "growth heartset"?

CHAPTER SIX:
THE FALSE JOY OF INDEPENDENCE

"It is not good that the man should be alone."
(Genesis 2:18)

Our culture has come to cherish independence in a way that few other cultures have. I'm not talking about **political** independence from a foreign power, which is generally a good thing. But I am talking about **personal** independence in the sense that we wish to answer to no one, to stand alone and be free from the burden of caring for one another.

In pop culture we hallow rugged individuals, solo flyers, and lone rangers. We work hard to remain free of any burdensome entanglement with anyone else. Our culture practically worships the principle of isolation.

Long ago I learned about the majestic California redwoods, which grow in groves because they have shallow root systems. These titans of the forest tower for hundreds of years, reaching up to 400 feet in height yet, astonishingly, have roots that descend less than 10 feet below the ground on average. How do they stand so tall for so long?

The answer is that redwoods always stand **together**. We never see a redwood reach its fullest potential apart from other redwoods. They only survive to maturity in groves, where their roots network together with other redwood roots to form a fabric foundation that can extend for hundreds of feet in any direction. In community, these majestic trees are able to stand for centuries without falling. They need each other to reach their highest potential.

Recently I learned about what botanists call the "Wood Wide Web". They have discovered that the function of root systems goes surprisingly deeper than simply providing a foundational structure. Scientists have learned that root systems are also able to share resources and even chemically "signal" one another about potential biological threats through a network of fungi.

It goes to further demonstrate what science is unveiling more and more: that all creation is interdependent; **nothing can long stand in isolation.** We were not designed for independence; we were designed by God to thrive in community. As the Lord Almighty said of Adam, *"It is not good for man to be alone." (Genesis 2:18)*

Of course, isolation, as an occasional practice, can be a very good thing. And while "getting away from it all" from time to time is a healing and restorative exercise, I fear that we sometimes elevate personal isolation to a dangerous position.

We **should** take a sabbath break now and then — last time I checked, setting aside one day a week for a holy sabbath was still one of the ten commandments!

We **should** enjoy the spiritual discipline of solitude from time to time. But if we redwoods pine for solitude too much, we risk being toppled by life's high winds and losing out on the holy joy of community.

We really do need each other.

Joy Restored: Directed Community

Joy cannot survive in perpetual seclusion. A house that prioritizes independence over community ultimately cannot stand.

In fact, from a Biblical perspective, quite the opposite is true: lasting joy, according to the wisdom of the Scriptures, is to be found only in the context of community. And not just any community.

Specifically, the word of God teaches us that we are designed to find our greatest strength, our greatest peace, our greatest joy *in community with God's people.*

Someone once said, *"If you want to go fast, go alone. If you want to go far, go together."* This is a wonderful saying in support of community. But it only tells half the story — it also matters *where* we are going together. If we are going far together in the direction of injustice and self-indulgence, that is not good. If our direction is toward the heart of God, that is very good.

Community is a powerful force, and it can serve either good or bad purposes. Locusts bring famine when they gather as a community. Termites destroy homes, crowds riot, people trample one another, and cults thrive... all on the general principle of community.

Community is not a virtue in and of itself. For a community to be healthy, it must be going in a healthy direction. The direction matters greatly. We must ask ourselves, where is our community headed? Where are the people *we identify as belonging to* going? Closer to God or farther and farther away from His love and truth? Up or down? We must choose the community we walk in very carefully.

For a follower of Jesus, the best option is clear: we belong to the body of Christ, to the family of God. We were made to belong to His church.

Oh, I know — churches are full of weird people. They can be awkward and stodgy. Churches, as a product of their parishioners, are not perfect, that is true. But a good church will always be focused on the primary goals of loving God and loving thy neighbor. Therefore, these strange little communities are part of God's design to lead us into all joy through participation in a healing community.

We might think we don't need the church. While that is possible, we must also consider that the church needs us. We not only grow best when we participate more fully in the family of God, we also share in the joy of encouraging others as they grow into maturity in Christ. As my inspired brother, Paul Bovee said to me after our church's Friday Fella's breakfast, "God has brought every one of us to this church for a reason."

Amen to that!

Forestry versus Selling Something

Some churches subscribe to the retail model of religious

community, where congregations are nothing more than crowds of consumers to be courted. Other churches subscribe to the forest model, where each individual benefits both from the community and while giving back to it through prayer, serving those in need, and encouraging others.

It isn't hard to tell the difference — when you walk into a church built on the retail model, they begin to **worship the worshippers** almost immediately. The messaging is clear: "Have a good time. Be comfortable."

As if to say, "It's all about you."

In a forest model church, the worship belongs to God alone. It's all about Him! We're not here to sell anything, rather to get to know and care for one another because that is the way God designed each of us to thrive. Each of us receives from one another, and each of us also gives to one another.

Of course, because churches are like families, there are bound to be people with whom we disagree. Sometimes there will be conflict. That doesn't mean we should opt out of participating in the family. We are human, and wherever flawed humans gather, they do flawed human things in flawed human ways. That's true in church as much as it's true in Congress, at work, school, and home.

The difference in the church is that we know we are **supposed** to be and do better. We are called to rise above our human nature and transcend our brokenness as God heals us — together. We are called to be holy, even though we are merely learning how.

The Principle of "One Another"

> *"And let us consider how to stir up one another*
> *to love and good works, not neglecting to meet together,*
> *as is the habit of some, but encouraging one another,*
> *and all the more as you see the Day drawing near."*
> *(Hebrews 10:24-25)*

When I was working my first full-time job out of high school, one of the other clerks at the grocery store explained to me that she believed in Jesus but didn't go to church because it wasn't necessary for salvation. She knew Jesus, she argued — even loved Him! So, what more could being part of a church help her know or do?

I was a very young Christian and didn't know how to respond, so I later went to an older believer, asked them what they thought and was told something I will never forget: "Steve, there are no 'Lone Rangers' in God's kingdom."

Then he opened the Scriptures to show me several "one another" verses - passage after passage in the New Testament that outline our **obligation** to one another. Here are just a few. As you read, look for these important two words: *"one another."*

*"Love **one another** with brotherly affection.*
*Outdo **one another** in showing honor."*
(Romans 12:10)

*"Therefore welcome **one another***
as Christ has welcomed you, for the glory of God."
(Romans 15:7)

"Finally, brothers, rejoice. Aim for restoration,
*comfort **one another**, agree with **one another**, live in peace;*
and the God of love and peace will be with you."
(2 Corinthians 13:11)

"For you were called to freedom, brothers.
Only do not use your freedom as an opportunity for the flesh,
*but through love serve **one another**."*
(Galatians 5:13)

*"Be kind to **one another**, tenderhearted,
forgiving one another, as God in Christ forgave you."
(Ephesians 4:32)*

*"And do not get drunk with wine, for that is debauchery, but
be filled with the Spirit, addressing **one another** in psalms and
hymns and spiritual songs, singing and making melody to the
Lord with your heart, giving thanks always and for everything
to God the Father in the name of our Lord Jesus Christ,"
(Ephesians 5:18-20)*

*"A new commandment I give to you,
that you love **one another**:
just as I have loved you,
you also are to love **one another**."
(John 13:34)*

*"By this all people will know that you are my disciples,
if you have love for **one another**."
(John 13:35)*

*"This is my commandment,
that you love **one another** as I have loved you."
(John 15:12)*

*"These things I command you,
so that you will love **one another**."
(John 15:17)*

This is just a sampling, there are more. But the important thing is that these "one another" verses are **not optional** — they are direct commands. We cannot say we love the Lord then refuse to do what He commands — and He commands us to diligently care for one another in community.

Simply believing in Jesus is not enough; if we believe in Him, we must obey Him as well. It is one thing to call Him Savior, but quite another to call Him Lord. Obedience to Jesus means that we embrace the sometimes difficult, but always beneficial, task of loving and serving one another.

What follows are just a few of the many, many joyful blessings that come from being involved in the community of God.

The Joy of Security

"Bear one another's burdens, and so fulfill the law of Christ." *(Galatians 6:2)*

Belonging to the family of God brings us the blessing of security in many practical ways.

We are exhorted by the word of God to "bear one another's burdens." How many times have we seen those who lose a job find work through connections in the church? How many times have we helped those with no food by providing a bag of groceries? How many of us know that if we lost everything, we would still have a place to lay our heads in a fellow believer's home because, in Jesus, we have friends who are closer than any of our earthly kin?

Belonging to the community of Christ brings the sacred blessing of security.

The Joy of Perspective

"Therefore, having put away falsehood, let each one of you speak the truth with his neighbor, for we are members one of another." (Ephesians 4:25)

Each individual opinion is incomplete. Great truths fanned into flame in the midst of a healing community are better than one malformed opinion smoldering in isolation. When we gather to worship, to fellowship, and to wrestle honestly with the word of God together, we bless one another with the wonderful gift of *perspective.*

This powerful perspective provided only in community is especially helpful when we face suffering and trials. Sometimes we are so close to a problem that we cannot see it clearly. When we are going through suffering that seems unbearable, it is an incomparable relief to meet with someone who has been there before — and, by the grace of God, come out stronger.

Belonging to the community of Christ brings us the joyful blessing of perspective.

The Joy of Belonging

"So we, though many, are one body in Christ,
and individually members one of another."
(Romans 10:25)

One of the greatest dangers of living in isolation is the sense that we don't belong anywhere. I have often wondered if there is a connection between the rising epidemic of depression and our misguided penchant for living in isolation.

When we indulge in the false joy of isolating ourselves — rather than being reminded on a regular basis of our significance and importance as members of God's family — we become easy targets for depression and self-doubt.

1 Peter 5:8 warns us to be watchful and alert for the devil who is like *"a roaring lion"* who seeks to devour the weak who stray from the flock. He is a sniper looking for an easy target. When we choose to walk alone, we practically place ourselves in his jaws.

In contrast, however, when we are committed to joining a community, especially the community of Jesus, we almost immediately find a deep sense of purpose and an unshakable sense that we are part of something bigger than ourselves. This is something no other community can offer.

Fully participating in the community of faith provides us with the holy joy of belonging.

Embracing Interdependence

If we are looking for joy by pursuing a life of independence, we will never find it. There is simply no lasting joy to be found in isolation.

Only when we embrace our interdependence, rather than our independence, can we experience all the joy life has to offer, for only in community can we find the joyful blessings of security, perspective, and belonging.

Are we meant to be Lone Rangers? I don't think so. The part of us that longs to ride the range alone also leaves us hopelessly vulnerable to the poison arrows of depression, purposelessness, and loneliness.

By the same token, if we are part of an unhealthy community — one that is headed in the wrong direction — it would be wise to move on while we still can.

Whatever the Lord may be saying to us right now, one thing is certain: there is a place and purpose for us — each of us — in His family.

We are each one of a kind.

No one else can take our place in the community of God.

We were made to find holy joy by belonging to God and to one another.

For Discussion:
When are you tempted to "go it alone?"
Which "one another" commandments in scripture stand most out to you?
Who can you encourage that tends to drift on the margins, outside of community?

CHAPTER SEVEN:
THE FALSE JOY OF TROPHIES

*"But whatever gain I had,
I counted as loss for the sake of Christ.
Indeed, I count everything as loss
because of the surpassing worth
of knowing Christ Jesus my Lord.
For his sake I have suffered the loss of all things
and count them as rubbish,
in order that I may gain Christ."
(Philippians 3:7-8)*

We find great yet short-lived joy in winning, accomplishments, and achievements.

Keith Luhnow is the grandfather of Brooke, my brother-in-law Robert's wife. A wise and caring man, Keith played football back in the 1960s, and he was very competitive. In one college game, Keith scored five touchdowns and ran 276 yards. He averaged an astonishing 158.9 yards-per-game rushing in 1961, setting a school record that stands to this day, nearly sixty years later! Keith was something of a phenomenon in Southern California.

That year, Keith was named an All-American college football player by the LA Times and was a draft pick for both the Oakland Raiders and San Francisco 49ers. He chose to play for the 49ers.

Keith knows a few things about the joy of winning! However, he was reminded once that the joy of winning, over time, proves to be a false joy — it is not complete and only temporary.

One day, his very young granddaughter, who happens to be a great athlete herself, was admiring some of his trophies — especially his All-American Award. As he stood proudly alongside her, she turned to him and said, "You know, Grandpa, I hate football."

Keith laughed when he told me the story — he knows his beloved granddaughter didn't mean any harm. Scarlett was simply speaking what was on her mind — like him, she loves many other sports, just isn't particularly fond of football. But the way she said it in her youthful innocence reminded him that our trophies won't always be celebrated, and they certainly don't guarantee *lasting joy*.

Trophies, winning, accomplishments, and achievements may, indeed, bring joy *for a season*, but that joy simply *does not remain*.

That is what Paul is getting at in Philippians 3:7-8.

Paul was a man of accomplishments — a man who could claim many of life's trophies, if you will. He lists several of his noteworthy achievements and credentials in the first few verses of Philippians 3, then goes on to declare that in his mind, they are all "rubbish" or, more literally "dung," compared with the greater prize of knowing Jesus.

Our winnings and achievements on earth may bring joy for a time. Yet when the entirety of our lives is accounted for, the skins we've won mean nothing at all in the light of the greater joy we have all been awarded in Christ Jesus. That is why Paul can boldly say of his trophies, *"For His sake I have suffered the loss of all things and count them as rubbish, in order that I may gain Christ." (v8b)*

The Dung File

My friend and mentor, Dennis Leggett, once shared the story of a graduate professor who kept a file labeled "Dung" in his cabinet. Tucked neatly away in that file were that distinguished professor's degrees, his noteworthy awards, the glowing accolades he had earned throughout the years. He was a dedicated Christian and didn't want to let his achievements go to his head. He wanted to make sure that he remembered, in spite of all of his earthly achievements, only one thing was truly worth glorying in: to *"gain Christ and be found in him." (v8b-9a)*

In Philippians 3:3, Paul says we *"glory in Christ Jesus and put no confidence in the flesh."* In other words, the triumph that matters is **not what I'm doing** but **what God is doing.** The real story is God's far greater victory of life over death being displayed *in me, with me,* and *through me,* not my twisted subplot of small human victories.

Holy Joy in the Quest

If lasting joy is not to be found in our earthly trophies, what is the point of pursuing them at all? Is it wrong to work hard in athletics, academics, at work or in our relationships?

Not at all! We were designed by God to achieve, to strive, to create.

Where would we be without scientists who work hard to discover new medicines, inventors who make our lives easier, and knowledge that helps us understand the world around us? Achievement can be a **good** thing — it is simply not the **best** thing.

According to Paul, **the best achievement** is to *"gain Christ and be found in Him."* (v8b,9a)

If we were created with an inner push to accomplish and obtain things that will bring us only temporary joy, is there any lasting joy at all to be found in the process?

I believe that we can experience holy joy even as we carry out our God-given prerogative to achieve the temporary trophies of this world. As we pursue the temporary victories of earthly achievements, we may yet find four-square joy **in the quest itself.**

To be more precise, **the lessons we learn on the journey** ultimately prove to be far more valuable than the earthly prizes we may win along the way. Indeed, the lessons we learn on the quest usually prove **even more valuable** when we earn **no earthly prize at all** — sometimes we **win**; sometimes we **learn.**

We don't win all the time. Most of us win only a fraction of the time! But each of us wins the greatest joy when we keep our eye on the overwhelming victory of becoming more like Christ as we travail. I believe this is what Paul is after when he states the strangest paradox of our faith — that we sometimes gain the greatest joy in our most bitter losses. In that sense, we are more than able to win eternal victories, even when we lose earthly accolades.

Here are three lasting joys just waiting to be discovered as we quest for the kingdom first.

The Joy of Fellowship

Among the most joyful and eternally significant prizes in life are the relationships we gain along the way. Whether we win or lose the trophies of earth, the friendships we make as we work, go to school, and raise our children together will outlast every paycheck, degree, and trophy.

We were designed by our maker to thrive in community with one another. As we busy ourselves rushing around to achieve more and more, let's not forget that one of the most sacred joys life has to offer is the gift of a lifelong friend.

"And let us consider how to stir up one another to love and good works" (Hebrews 10:24)

The Joy of Growing

Growth takes place most quickly in times of adversity. Weightlifters know that **resistance** is the key to developing muscle. Climbing uphill develops endurance and expands lung capacity. Every step along life's path offers an opportunity to learn something new and to grow. We just need to be willing to accept the challenge.

If this is true physically and mentally, it is **even more true spiritually.** When we keep our sights set on the higher prize of what God is doing — even as we pursue earthly accomplishments — our spiritual growth will skyrocket. One of the greatest joys we can experience comes from the transformation of heart, soul, mind, and strength into the likeness of Christ. Jesus is always teaching us new ways to trust, new ways to serve, and new ways to grow.

"You have heard; now see all this;
and will you not declare it? From this time forth I announce
to you new things, hidden things that you have not known."
(Psalm 48:6)

The Joy of Virtue

We live in a time when virtue is taking a beating. Many people today value winning over morality; gain over godliness. But we know that God is more pleased with virtue than winning.

When it comes to winning, most people will set aside morality — and therefore the author of morality — in order to come out on top, believing the ends justify the means.

Into this season of self-promotion and dogged clawing our way to the top, the Lord asks us, "Where's the profit in it?" What does it profit us to gain more trophies, to make more fortune — to win earthly power at the cost of losing our souls?

What will people remember more — the things we accomplish or the wicked things we did to accomplish them? Which trophy will last longer — the prize of a short-sighted victory at the expense of personal integrity or the joy of running with endurance the race marked out for us by the Spirit?

What we do is not as important to God as how we do it.

In a season of political waste, I am reminded of the words of Jesus: "No bad tree can bear good fruit." We must pray for our leaders to come under holy conviction — to understand that their accomplishments will crumble if they do not establish themselves in the ways of righteousness.

Any gains made at the expense of morality and virtue will always be short lived. Indeed, history shows us that the more a leader compromises their ethical standards to accomplish their agendas, the more quickly those accomplishments will be undone.

Lasting joy is not found in winning but in developing Godly virtue as we press ahead.

"Keep your conduct among the Gentiles honorable,
so that when they speak against you as evildoers, they may see
your good deeds and glorify God on the day of visitation."
(1 Peter 2:12)

Signing Off

I've never been a star athlete or scholar, but I have tasted the fleeting joy of achievement and winning.

I can be a bit reckless. At 19 years-old, halfway through my sophomore year — much to the shock of my parents — I dropped out of college in San Diego.

I had felt a sincere and irresistible call to do something I was completely unequipped for — to start a Christian radio ministry in my hometown of Carlsbad, New Mexico. I believed that a radio station playing "Jesus music" and a message of hope could have an enormous impact.

So, joining a long procession of other reckless individuals throughout history, I said, "Here I am, Lord. Use me."

Many small miracles happened, and, purely by the grace of God, K-Dove was established and operating in just a few short months. I returned to college in the fall, having started a non-profit corporation, organized an amazing board of directors, and listened to Jesus music actually playing on the air. That little radio ministry lasted for more than a decade, and, from what I hear, it made a difference.

I will always consider that to be a great accomplishment. It is a trophy I cherish.

However, K-Dove is off the air now. In time, the internet and satellite radio came along. Larger Christian radio stations stretched their networks all the way to that remote corner of New Mexico.

A few years ago, on the way out of town after a rare homecoming to visit my father, the GPS took me right by the old radio tower. I had to stop and reflect. I got out and laid on the hood of my car, watching the red lights slowly fade in and then out again against the early morning starry sky — just as I had nearly thirty years before.

As the red lights shone and then dissipated, I was reminded that our earthly victories do the same. The achievements I relished once upon a time had been long forgotten.

I'm not sad, though. Just the opposite — remembering that experience still brings me great joy.

Why? Because God had much bigger plans for me than starting a radio ministry that year. He pushed me to grow and learn new skills that have been essential to my ministry since then. I learned that virtue in business dealings is far more important than a winning hand.

Most importantly, He restored my relationship with my parents.

My mother and I reconciled after a few very bitter years — from friction I had caused between us. It was the last meaningful time I would spend with her before she passed away from cancer a few years later.

Also, that same summer, my father suggested we attend a Christian men's retreat together in Boulder, Colorado. He recommitted his life and his marriage to Jesus, and we shared a deep spiritual connection from that time on. Later, my mother would privately tell me that after the retreat he had finally become the man she had always hoped he would be.

Today, the old forgotten trophy of 1993 — the radio station — means practically nothing to anyone. But the holy joys of restored fellowship, personal growth, and lessons on virtue still shine brightly.

Such lights — such joys — do not fade.

Casting Down our Golden Crowns

There is a beautiful passage in the book of Revelation where the faithful in Christ cast their trophies at the feet of Jesus.

"[And] the twenty-four elders fall down before him who is seated on the throne and worship him who lives forever and ever. They cast their crowns before the throne, saying, 'Worthy are you, our Lord and God, to receive glory and honor and power, for you created all things, and by your will they existed and were created.'"
(Revelation 4:9-11)

May we have the wisdom to join their procession, knowing that all earthly crowns are nothing compared to the **surpassing joy** of *"gaining Christ and being found in Him."*

For Discussion:
Who do you know that is perhaps forgotten, or maybe has not "accomplished" much in the world's eyes, but is still joyful?
Why do we so easily forget the victories of the past?
In what ways can you remind yourself that your greatest victory is being loved by God?

CHAPTER EIGHT:
THE FALSE JOY OF SAFETY

"In the world you will have tribulation.
But take heart; I have overcome the world."
(John 16.33)

One of my favorite television shows of the early 2000s was "Dirty Jobs" hosted by Mike Rowe. Rowe would visit different job sites and do the grunt work that had to be done in order to keep society moving along. The show gave us a glimpse into every awful job you could imagine, from sewer maintenance to hog farming to garbage collection.

Rowe had a saying that I came to appreciate: "Safety first — or at least top five." He had a point: some jobs would never get done if we really made safety our number one priority. Safety cannot always be first — if it were, some of us would never go to work, much less drive on the freeway or raise children!

Some things are worth risking our safety for.

Yet, despite life being inherently risky, we live in a culture **obsessed** with safety.

Warning labels alert us to endless safety threats all around. Think of the products we buy and their warning labels. It seems as though every object in our home, from the baby's pacifier to the pillows we sleep on, comes with the threat of imminent death should we use it improperly.

Most people assume safety to be a basic human right, calling in the lawyers for even the smallest accidents. Safety is often touted as the highest value in the workplace, school, and household.

Of course, I admit that safety matters, especially in the physical realm. Without safety-first policies, most dangerous work would never get done today. I have a friend who is a highly-regarded expert in the field of ergonomics. He is often called in as an expert witness when an accident leads to a court trial. In fact, a number of the warning labels we so often see have come about from cases he's worked on! My friend has a very important job, sometimes with life-or-death consequences.

I certainly don't want to downplay the importance of safety!

But while I agree that safety is **an important** value, from a spiritual perspective it cannot become **the most important** value.

The Fog of Fear

Sadly, people of faith are not immune to this perennial fog of fearfulness. We know too many Christians who refuse to go out into the world, preferring instead the safety of hiding behind rose-colored stained-glass windows, offering prayers for a dying world outside — but refusing to bless it by intentionally stepping outside into the fray and bearing the gospel of peace.

For those who prefer to tuck themselves away in the supposed safety of the church and choose to fellowship only with those who act, think, and vote like themselves, I respectfully say: you must think your God is a wimp.

The God we serve is not intimidated by the world He created or anything in it. Only a cowering, musclebound God would be scared. If we allow our fear of those who are different from us to dominate our relationships, we must have a frail faith indeed.

How many would-be Christians cower in life's corner instead of standing boldly in the center of the fire, assured of God's presence and empowerment? The world is not always safe — that is true. Yet God is not at all afraid and, therefore, neither should we be much afraid. God promises to be with us as we follow Him — but not that we will necessarily be safe from all earthly danger.

Real Joy Requires Real Risk

When we have been wounded by life, we understandably tend to shy away from the risks that ultimately make life worth living. But real joy cannot be found by hiding in the caves of relative safety.

Indeed, to exist is to risk. The most important developments in history have been predicated on it. Early explorers first charted the globe at great risk to life and limb. What about the risk Jonas Salk took by testing the polio vaccine on himself? Or that which Dr. Martin Luther King Jr took by choosing nonviolent protest instead of violence?

These are modern examples. What about some examples from the Biblical halls of faith?

Where would we be if Abraham had not risked his safety and heeded the voice of the God who called him to chance everything familiar in Haran and journey to an unseen promised land?

Where would the Hebrews have been if Moses had not risked his life to confront Pharaoh? What would have happened if the little boy David had not risked getting squashed when he stood up to Goliath or Paul had not risked shipwrecks, beatings, whippings and even being stoned to death for the sake of sharing the good news of God's love?

And, of course, the capstone — the greatest risk ever taken in the history of the universe was the risk God took when He came to earth as a poor, Middle-Eastern infant who became a man, crucified under Pontius Pilate, only to rise again in fulfillment of the Scriptures.

We know why God risked so much — *it was for joy* — the joy of loving us.

We see that nearly everything worthwhile requires some risk. Safety cannot be our top priority, or we will never experience anything but false joys.

We must not be fooled by a world that tells us the best path is the safest one. That is a lie. The best path is the one God lays out for us — regardless of the risks involved.

Speaking of Warning Labels and Disclaimers...

I would be remiss at this point if I said that taking **unnecessary** risks was a good idea. Some risks are just plain foolish. Of course, we should take reasonable precautions in life. We should wear seat belts, eat healthy foods, avoid making toast while taking a bath, etc.

Risk for risk's sake is pointless, and many risks serve no higher purpose. When I advocate for calculated risk-taking, I am only talking about those that are worthwhile.

It should go without saying that needless suffering is to be avoided — while the often-dirty job of standing for the truth will require taking risks that might lead to suffering. Yet we can rest assured that any suffering we may experience for the cause of Christ is never in vain. In fact, God even works through our suffering for His purposes to cause us to grow in hope and rediscover lasting joy!

As Paul says:

> *"Not only that, but we rejoice in our sufferings, knowing that suffering produces endurance, and endurance produces character, and character produces hope" (Romans 5:3-4)*

Three Risks Worth Taking

> *"He has shown you, O man, what is good;*
> *And what does the Lord require of you*
> *But to do justly,*
> *To love mercy,*
> *And to walk humbly with your God"*
> *(Micah 6:8 - NKVJ)*

These three "good" things — justice, mercy, and faith — can actually be quite risky. Doing the right thing (doing justly) gets people killed every day. Showing mercy also comes with great risk — what if the person I forgive hurts me again? And certainly, the record number of martyrdoms in the past several decades have shown us, without question, that it is extremely dangerous to walk humbly with our God.

If we take this challenge from Micah to heart — to do justly, love mercy, and walk humbly with God — we will inherently expose ourselves to great risk. None of these three admonitions could be called safe — yet each one is a prerequisite to experiencing holy joy.

The Joyful Risk of Doing Justly

Doing justly means both **being good** and **doing good**. It has to do with being a just person, or, as some English translations render it, "righteous." Biblical righteousness and justice are often functionally the same concept. This requires both personal virtue (living a moral life that is above reproach) and also social justice (caring for those in need who have no voice).

Being good means risking being teased, scorned, and ostracized for taking a position on moral issues. When we take a stand for personal morality, we open ourselves to being labeled a wet blanket, a prude, or narrow-minded. It takes courage to "be good" in a world that rewards evildoers. But it is much better to stand on the high ground of personal morality than to sink into the quicksand of unrestrained flesh.

Doing good, on the other hand, means risking being hurt, taken advantage of, and accused of having ulterior motives. When we stretch out our hands to serve others, we are always taking a risk that the people we are helping won't appreciate it, receive it, or change.

Being generous and charitable, like our Father in Heaven, is inherently very risky business. What if the person I am helping uses my handout to buy alcohol or drugs? What if this assistance is taken for granted? What if the person I'm trying to help refuses to change?

While these are valid questions — and even though experience might teach us that serving others often leads to disappointing results — we are still compelled by our Lord Jesus Christ to take the risk, serve the least of His children, and live sacrificially the way He did.

Perhaps the best way to deal with our doubts about serving others is to remember how God has been so good to us, even while we have been stubbornly opposed to Him. God's blessings are showered on the just and the unjust alike, and Jesus is our example. As He has treated us, so should we treat one another.

"Pure and undefiled religion before God and the Father is this: to visit orphans and widows in their trouble, and to keep oneself unspotted from the world."
(James 1:27)

"And let us not grow weary of doing good, for in due season we will reap, if we do not give up."
(Galatians 6:9)

The Joyful Risk of Mercy

Micah 6:8 continues by reminding us that one of the requirements of holy joy is to show mercy to those who injure us. This means that we must be kind and forgiving when the world would counsel us to retaliate.

What could be riskier than forgiveness? What if we are hurt again after we've forgiven the person who trespasses against us? We might easily convince ourselves that it would be far safer not to forgive and linger with our grudges, clinging to them until our last bitter breath. But what kind of life would that be?

Forgiveness puts the forgiver at risk — always. Our sister or brother may sin against us yet another seventy times seven. There is no guarantee that forgiving someone will mean that they never hurt us again.

Loving mercy is not safe.

Whatever our reservations about showing mercy and kindness to others may be, the risk is well worth the potential return. We might not see it happen the first, second — or even the 490th time — but in the end, mercy triumphs over judgment. The God who brings final justice will be our advocate one day. For now, we are simply called to take the risk of loving mercy.

To live with unresolved anger is no life at all. Loving mercy means that we must have the courage to let go of our past hurts and move on.

> *"Then Peter came up and said to him,*
> *'Lord, how often will my brother sin against me,*
> *and I forgive him? As many as seven times?'*
> *"Jesus said to him, 'I do not say to you seven times,*
> *but seventy-seven times.'"*
> *(Matthew 18.21-22)*

The Joyful Risk of Walking Humbly with God

Finally, it may seem contradictory in cultures where we have a measure of religious freedom, but those who walk humbly with God today know how dangerous it can be. It is always very risky to stand for absolute truth.

For example, bring nearly any book to school or work, no matter how profane or shocking, and people will praise and admire your intellectual bravery. Bring a Bible to work or school, and you will be immediately shunned as narrow-minded.

Our culture is not as enlightened as it thinks it is. Narrow-minded people still walk narrow-minded streets in great numbers. Lopsided opinions pass for diversity, when they are, in actuality, merely edge voices that seek to exclude all dissent.

If we do walk with God, even as humbly as we ought to, we will be judged by a relativistic culture that cannot stand any system that claims objective truth. And so, we are left with a choice: to retreat from the world in the name of "safety" or walk humbly into the fire with God at our side. To walk with God means to risk being condemned by the world.

A word about nonviolent resistance: while some who claim the flag of Christ have indeed been reckless in their rhetoric and hateful in their deeds — and thus as narrow-minded as the world — the vast majority of us simply wish to believe what we believe and not be unfairly shunned for holding ourselves and our homes to higher moral standards.

We are to be bold in our walk with God, of course. But we have no business being hateful or unkind to those with whom we disagree. Christlike boldness does not abide the absence of kindness. Our boldness is to be a testimony to the world — but the even greater testimony must be our attitude of love for God, one another, and especially our enemies.

"Keep alert with all perseverance,
making supplication for all the saints, and also for me,
that words may be given to me in opening my mouth boldly to
proclaim the mystery of the gospel,
for which I am an ambassador in chains,
that I may declare it boldly,
as I ought to speak."
(Ephesians 6.18b-20)

May doing what is right, loving mercy, and walking humbly with God become more important to us than our own personal safety.

Holy joy is worth the risk.

For Discussion:
Can you think of an example when safety might not be the most important value?
Can there be true rewards without real risks?
Is following God really and truly risky?

CHAPTER NINE:
THE FALSE JOY OF CHASING KNOWLEDGE

"Trust in the Lord with all your heart,
and do not lean on your own understanding.
In all your ways acknowledge him,
and he will make straight your paths.
Be not wise in your own eyes;
fear the Lord, and turn away from evil.
It will be healing to your flesh
and refreshment to your bones."
(Proverbs 3:5-8)

Recently, I visited the great secular temple to knowledge, the Library of Congress in Washington D.C. In the awe-inspiring reading room, an enormous rotunda encircles readers below, hiding them under the shadows of statues of Shakespeare, Isaac Newton, Moses, and other great figures in humanity's "Knowledge Hall of Fame." Inscriptions on the walls throughout the building extol knowledge as the highest achievement of humankind.

I, respectfully, disagree. The highest knowledge we can attain today will prove to be riddled with errors and omissions tomorrow. The pure pursuit of knowledge may bring satisfaction for a while, but eventually it proves to be a false joy.

Many people believe that joy can be found by simply acquiring knowledge. While it is true that a college degree can improve income and open opportunities, it is not necessarily true that the pursuit of knowledge brings greater joy in life. Many college professors suffer from bitter hopelessness, living lives devoid of joy in spite of their extensive knowledge.

There is also a kind of bigotry that comes with knowledge — not in the sense of racism or sexism, but in the original sense of bigotry, which is any entrenched, heels-dug-in, sense that "by God, I'm right and nothing will change my mind." In that sense, bigotry plagues us all when we are so convinced we are right that we are blind to our own weakness.

While knowledge is profoundly useful and clearly beneficial, it is not the key to lasting joy. One need look no further than the beaming face of a child with a developmental disability to realize that great joy can be found apart from the burden of knowledge.

Knowledge's Folly

The problem with the pursuit of knowledge — and the reason it cannot produce lasting joy — is that there is always something more to learn. Modern degree programs and instructional institutions tend to prey upon the false hopes of students who suppose they will know **everything** if they simply learn **some things**. But knowledge changes as rapidly as technology advances. Even if we know "everything" today, tomorrow we will not.

As anyone who has earned a genuine education can tell you, the quest for knowledge generally leaves us with two things: great debt and surprisingly little joy!

The pursuit of knowledge leaves many of us highly arrogant while acutely insecure. Arrogance is due to feeling falsely superior to our brethren. Insecure because a good education reveals that we are dots, peering at other distant dots — how little we actually know about the universe!

Education versus Indoctrination

I must say a word here about today's unfortunate mislabeling of indoctrination as education. Indoctrination is not the same as education. The two are very different. Getting a certificate or a degree, which is the payout for completing a course of instruction, should never be confused with getting an education.

Indoctrination is the cold memorization of facts — or, more often, opinions.

Education is the discovery of truth.

Indoctrination clutters our heads with imbalanced trivia while education seeks to dismantle our preconceptions so that we may **learn how to learn**.

Indoctrination desires to trim the corners of truth to stuff it neatly into a closed case, while education desires to *unclose* cases to get at the deepest truths.

Unfortunately, there are some fear-based factions prowling the realm of Christendom that shun the value of education. Christianity driven by faith — as opposed to Christianity cornered by fear — is invigorated by the discovery of science and truth, not because it believes it can button down every truth but because it wants to touch more and more of the fabric of God's infinitely expanding creation.

Indoctrination seeks to pin down the edges of God, while education keeps discovering more and more of His revelation to explore.

With authentic education, every door we open leads to ten more. While this ever-expanding nature of education may be unsettling at first, for a true Christian seeking hard after truth, it actually brings greater comfort to our faith because it reinforces our belief that God — and His creation, by extension — is indeed much bigger than we can fully define or pin down.

The pursuit of knowledge, although good and healthy, is ultimately a chasing after an uncatchable wind. Like the modern skeptics C.S. Lewis, Josh McDowell, and Lee Strobel — who each came to God through fierce questioning and doubt — believers do not need to fear hard questions and rigorous research. God's word and His promises hold up! Ask all the questions. Seek all the answers. Do not be afraid to beat down Heaven's door.

Joy Restored: Accepting Mystery

"Truly, I say to you, unless you turn and become like children,
you will never enter the kingdom of heaven."
(Matthew 18:3)

How might we find true joy as we go about the God-given task of learning, even as we run into the disappointing limitations of human knowledge? Can we experience true joy even as we discover how small our minds really are?

I love and appreciate science and what it brings to our lives. From air conditioning to air travel, from agricultural science feeding the world's hungry to medical science adding precious tomorrows to children's lives — I am grateful for the advancements God has allowed us to make in the sciences.

Scientists are uncovering new interactions daily between the most minute parts of the cell. I've seen a chart of the interactions they have been able to map between nuclei and mitochondria, transmembrane conductors and cytoplasm, and dozens of other parts. The concept is far beyond my comprehension level — to me it all resembles a Tokyo subway map!

While brilliant minds have been able to prove that each component in a cell communicates mysteriously with many other components, in many cases, we don't quite understand how or why. It seems that every time researchers are able to map one interaction, they discover ten more! Understanding these interactions may lead to cures for Alzheimer's and diabetes. What a wonder!

But it strikes me that, as these scientists examine creation more and more closely, they find that far more exists in the universe than previous generations of scientists thought possible. Instead of eliminating mystery, their research discovers **more and more mystery** every day. The mystery grows, rather than resolves. The case doesn't close, it opens deeper and wider the closer we look.

The key to restoring joy as we encounter the limits of human knowledge is to get acquainted with an important concept of faith: *embracing mystery.*

Mystery is not the absence of meaning but the presence of more truth than our senses can currently perceive. Accepting mystery is essential to finding holy joy.

How can someone be crucified — dead and buried — only to rise again on the third day? It's a mystery. We acknowledge that there is more to the universe than we can understand in our limited existence. We believe in things we cannot see, touch, or taste with our senses because we are comfortable with mystery. Faith believes there is more to reality than we can sense with our eyes — and those things we cannot see, we receive and *enjoy* as mysteries.

In other words, true joy is only possible in the context of pursuing knowledge when we surrender our arrogance and recognize that we will only ever know very little indeed. When we accept mystery as a normal part of our human experience — become unafraid to admit we have *so much to learn* — then we become like children again.

To restore the joy of mystery, we have to get comfortable with our limitations. What follows are three limitations I am, personally, coming to accept.

Our Viewpoint is Essentially Monospect, Not Circumspect

> *"O Lord, what is man that you regard him,*
> *or the son of man that you think of him?"*
> *(Psalm 144:3)*

Being "circumspect" means seeing all around us, able to observe every possible angle. Being "monospect," on the other hand, means recognizing that our own perception is merely one perspective, and a very limited one at that. As much as we might try to convince ourselves that we are circumspect — that we can comprehend every side of an issue — the truth is that we are all limited to just one vantage point: our own.

We should strive to "walk circumspectly" as the Scriptures suggest (Ephesian 5:15), but our ability to actually **achieve** circumspection is very limited.

Even if we were to study for a lifetime, we would never see the truth from every possible angle. Therefore, we need to be honest with ourselves, accepting that we won't know everything there is to know about **any** subject. Even the leading expert in an area of knowledge is only a beginner, limited by their singular experience and perspective.

To experience true joy in our pursuit of knowledge, we must become comfortable with the mystery that our perspective is only **monospective** — our ability to understand creation will be limited by the confines of our linear existence.

Our Consciousness is Microniscient, Not Omniscient

"'Who is this that hides counsel without knowledge?'
Therefore I have uttered what I did not understand,
things too wonderful for me, which I did not know."
(Job 42:3)

If "omniscience" means knowing all, "microniscience" means knowing very little. Only God is omniscient. Joy comes when we embrace the mystery of our microniscience. Even the wisest of us is only a novice — the most knowledgeable among us only a beginner. It is refreshing to think that, as much as we know, we are still only scratching the surface.

As we pursue knowledge, let us always keep in mind that everything we come to know will ultimately remain limited. Our fullest capacity for understanding barely amounts to a glimpse of eternal truth — our worldview represents only a whisper of what is real. By embracing our "microniscience," we can discover true joy as we explore truth on earth.

Our Vision is Microscopic, Not Macroscopic

*"Oh, the depth of the riches and wisdom and knowledge
of God! How unsearchable are his judgments
and how inscrutable his ways!"*
(Romans 11:33)

Microscopes are used to view a minuscule section of a very narrow slice of reality. Having a "microscopic" world view means zooming in on a very narrow experience of reality. A microscopic person only looks at what is directly in front of them with no regard for the incredible vastness of the Almighty God's expansive creation. A microscopic person is fearful of truth that may extend off the slide, outside their view, beyond their limited understanding.

In contrast, being "macroscopic" means having the ability to step back and recognize that a bigger picture exists. The stitching on a ball is not all there is to a baseball game. While a microscopic mind is forgetful of history and doomed to repeat the tragic mistakes of the past, a macroscopic mind is mindful of the lessons learned from past mistakes and seeks to grow into the fullness of the wisdom of God.

Mystery's Victory

Accepting mystery is not admitting defeat but acknowledging our limitations. Embracing mystery is not giving up on learning but accepting the challenge that there is always more to be understood. Science and faith are not in conflict, instead they are complementary disciplines. Science investigates truth; faith interprets it.

Those believers who feel threatened by the discovery of truth misunderstand the essence of faith. Faith is not afraid of truth bigger than ourselves. In fact, genuine faith knows that all truth belongs to God – and therefore, **rejoices** in the unsearchable nature of it.

"Now to him who is able to strengthen you according to my
gospel and the preaching of Jesus Christ,
according to the revelation of the mystery that was kept
secret for long ages but has now been disclosed and through
the prophetic writings has been made known to all nations,
according to the command of the eternal God,
to bring about the obedience of faith — to the only wise God
be glory forevermore through Jesus Christ! Amen."
(Romans 16:25-27)

Lord, the only Wise God, please help us to see how small we truly are — and to seek joy, not in knowing much, as much as in being known by You!

For Discussion:
What are some of the benefits of knowledge?
If someone loses their mental capacity, how can they still be a disciple of Jesus?
What are the essential things we need to know in order to be happy in life?

CHAPTER TEN:
THE FALSE JOY OF VICTIMHOOD

"So we do not lose heart.
Though our outer self is wasting away,
our inner self is being renewed day by day.
For this light momentary affliction is preparing for us
an eternal weight of glory beyond all comparison,
as we look not to the things that are seen
but to the things that are unseen."
(2 Corinthians 4:16-18a)

Munchausen syndrome is an attention craving disorder. It is when someone inflicts wounds or pain on themselves in order to gain medical attention. Called a *"factitious"* disorder - it is classified as a genuine mental illness.

A more sinister variation of this mental disorder, known as "Munchausen by proxy," is when the person craving attention inflicts pain on someone they care for, either a child or an elderly ward, in order to be seen as a heroic caregiver and secure attention from the medical community. Far from being a rare disorder, in my experience as a pastor I have counseled more than a few who dabble in the dark art of relishing the role of "victim" to their own — or a loved one's — detriment.

We all face the temptation to pity ourselves, to use our pain as a way to gain attention and pity from others. Playing the victim in life isn't necessarily a sign of mental illness — perhaps it is simply a case of human nature left unchecked.

When Adam fell, we all fell. When he lost innocence, we all lost innocence. We had it made in the garden of our youth, but, as the poet Robert Frost observed: nothing gold can stay.

Nature's first green is gold,
Her hardest hue to hold.
Her early leaf's a flower;
But only so an hour.
Then leaf subsides to leaf.
So Eden sank to grief,
So dawn goes down to day.
Nothing gold can stay.
(Robert Frost, Nothing Gold Can Stay)

Adam and Eve could have remained in grief forever about their lost innocence, playing the victim outside the fiery Garden gate, doing nothing but feeling sorry for themselves until they returned to clay and dust.

But, while their grief was real and warranted, God afforded them no such pity party. He gave them work to do. He gave them a mandate to be fruitful and multiply by shaping the soil and raising children. Even as the sun set on the Garden, a glimmer of hope remained — a hint of golden promise in the fading light. The Lord does nothing without a plan, and even as Eden lost its luster, He was working to provide an opportunity for us to, one day, experience innocence restored.

We still grieve the pain of lost innocence — both Adam's rebellion against God, which forever warped our DNA, and our own personal rebellions, which have led us down many roads pocked with pain.

It's How You Place the Blame

Who knows where suffering comes from? Only God can account for all of it. It would be easy to blame someone else for the times we are wounded along life's journey. Certainly, other people are responsible for some of our pain. But we also bring pain upon ourselves when we pluck the apple of our own accord and sink our teeth into flesh we were warned about long ago.

Whether we regret more the foolish things **we have done** or the good things **we wish we had done** is hard to say.

But here's my point: suffering is inevitable. Pain is a part of life. Wounds, injuries, and insults will not cease until the Lord Jesus Christ returns to open the Garden gate once again and make all things new in Heaven, on Earth, and in our hearts.

It is one thing to **experience** pain and quite another to **become** our pain. Some of us wear our pain too proudly — we like the attention it brings and the pathos it produces. Rather than avoiding pain, we can become professional victims, looking for reasons to be offended or hurt — all to enthrone our misery and seek to be the center of others' attention.

Joy Restored: Overcoming our Pain

For a follower of Jesus, pain is not something to **inhabit** and **become** but something to **conquer** and **overcome**. In Romans 8 Paul reminds us:

> *Who shall separate us from the love of Christ?*
> *Shall tribulation, or distress, or persecution,*
> *or famine, or nakedness, or danger, or sword?*
> *As it is written, "For your sake*
> *we are being killed all the day long;*
> *we are regarded as sheep to be slaughtered."*
> *(Romans 8:5-36 KJV)*

If he ended there, we could call Paul the greatest attention-seeking victim of all. But brother Paul stops after this complaint. Suffering is real, yes, but it must never be the end of the story. Observe the force with which Paul continues:

> *"No, in all these things we are more than conquerors*
> *through him who loved us.*
> *For I am sure that neither death nor life,*
> *nor angels nor rulers,*
> *nor things present nor things to come,*
> *nor powers, nor height nor depth,*

nor anything else in all creation,
will be able to separate us
from the love of God
in Christ Jesus our Lord."
(Romans 8:37-39)

Paul says we are **more than** — not **merely** — conquerors of pain. He flashes before us every example of trial and tribulation he can think of — dark angels, vicious rulers, trials of today, trials of tomorrow, and the torment of every other created thing — then urges us to rise above all of them.

Instead of **becoming** our pain and playing the victim, Paul says that true joy comes when we **overcome** our pain, seeing every affliction for what it is: light and momentary. True joy is a matter of keeping a heavenly perspective as we endure earthly suffering.

Three Responses to Pain

So how do we find lasting joy when suffering comes our way? As a starting point, remember that nobody simply **finds** joy. We must **choose it** by choosing a spiritual vantage point.

Joy never randomly occurs. Joy is a volitional act. It is not happenstance. Those who wait for joy to arrive have already missed the train. Joy must be hunted and captured. Joy is a fearless, risk-ready act of the will that decides to forsake the temporary, false joy of playing the victim, and choosing the true, holy joy which looks for the love of God in all things.

We have three basic options when we face trials of various kinds: We can choose to live in denial, choose to play the victim, or we can choose to be victorious. Each option opens into a path, and each path leads to a different destination. God has given us the freedom to choose for ourselves. God has also saddled us with the responsibility of bearing the consequences of our choices.

Denial: Ignoring Pain

"I have said these things to you, that in me you may have peace. In the world you will have tribulation. But take heart; I have overcome the world." (John 16:33)

Paul describes a rather bleak picture of the life of faith in 2 Corinthians 4: It is hardly the stuff of Fifth Avenue advertising for the newly minted life of a Christian. He says the followers of Jesus are "afflicted in every way", "perplexed", "persecuted", "struck down", "always being given over to death". How would any of those look as advertisements for the life of faith? Not good. Certainly not easy.

Paul doesn't pretend that following Jesus means the end of hardship or trouble in life. If anything, he is living proof that following Jesus exposes us to even more trouble and strife as we take our stand in opposition to the ways of the world and go against the flow. And we know what happens when we go against the flow — we bump into things... ***hard things!***

So, what good news is there in all of this? While Paul doesn't frost our cakes with lazy pie in the sky preaching, he does point out that suffering is not the end of the story for a heart set on seeking the joy of God beyond the barricade.

We are afflicted in every way, yes, "but not crushed". We are perplexed and without answers, "but not driven to despair." We may be persecuted, but we are never "forsaken;" struck down, but never ever "destroyed." We are "always being given over to death" — but even our dying is a sacrament — we are living sacrifices offered "for Jesus' sake, so that the life of Jesus also may be manifested in our mortal flesh."

Paul does not say pain is ***absent*** in the life of a disciple — it is redeemed.

In Jesus, all our affliction is given the holy purpose of stirring those about us to witness the power and glory of God at work in the catastrophes of our lives. When our eyes cease to focus on our pain and are instead set on obedience to the way of Christ, even the harshest critics cannot help but shut their mouths and marvel at such a mystery.

Even the most bitter suffering cannot take away the holy joy of a soul whose eyes are fixed on Jesus.

Victimhood: Worshiping Pain

Have you ever known someone who loves their pain so much that they really don't want to let go of it? There is a story of, perhaps, just such a man in John chapter 5. Jesus encounters a paraplegic lying next to the Pool of Bethesda in Jerusalem. When we read the story, it is obvious that this poor man needs to be healed in order to walk again. Yet when He meets the lame man, Jesus asks him a very strange question:

> *"When Jesus saw him lying there*
> *and knew that he had already been there a long time,*
> *he said to him,*
> *'Do you want to be healed?'"*
> *(John 5:6)*

"Do you want to be healed"?

Really? Isn't it obvious, Jesus?

I believe that by asking that particular question, Jesus is getting at the heart of victimhood in each of us. Do we really want to be healed? Or do we just want to wallow in pity and absorb the attention of others in order to feed an unhealthy and unholy desire?

And so it goes for each one of us. Jesus is asking the question, as we lay on our mats beside the pools of healing we can never quite bring ourselves to touch.

"Do you want to be healed? Do you really want victory over the past? Because I can give it to you. But if you want to remain a victim, there is nothing I can do for you. The choice is yours, my child."

Whether it is the perpetual sting of a chronic disease or the bitterness of regret, we all know the temptation to remain in our pain and choose to be a victim instead. Jesus, however, sees right through our apathy, and He asks us today, again: do we really want to be healed?

Victory: Giving Pain to God

Being a victor instead of a victim is both the hardest choice to make and the easiest. It is the hardest because it requires letting go of our darling victimhood. It is the easiest because it requires absolutely no effort on our part.

In fact, like all grace from God, there is nothing required from us other than surrender. The hardest part of faith is letting go of our burdens. The easiest part of faith is letting God carry it. His yoke is easy, and His burden is light because He does all the heavy lifting. All we must do is walk with Him daily, surrendering each pain, bravely confronting our denial, and forever relinquishing our victimhood to Him.

When we humble ourselves by giving our burdensome grief and anxiety to Jesus, the sweetest victory is all ours.

"Humble yourselves, therefore, under the mighty hand of God so that at the proper time he may exalt you, casting all your anxieties on him, because he cares for you."
(1 Peter 5:6-7)

Pain's Empowering Potential

Which will it be for us? Denial, victimhood, or victory? In spite of my temptations, I know which one I have come to prefer. Every wound is pregnant with purpose.

Trials have unmatched potential to:

Strengthen us by teaching us to rely on the strength of God.

Give us a battle to fight by focusing our attention on injustice in the world.

And, most importantly, **point others to the hope that can only come from God.**

There is joy more real than the sting of this world's suffering. There is joy that far surpasses this world's sorrow. Trials will come and go, but the joy that comes from surrendering all to God will stand forever.

"Since we have the same spirit of faith according to what has been written, 'I believed, and so I spoke,' we also believe, and so we also speak, knowing that he who raised the Lord Jesus will raise us also with Jesus and bring us with you into his presence. For it is all for your sake, so that as grace extends to more and more people it may increase thanksgiving, to the glory of God. (2 Corinthians 4:13-15)

For Discussion:
Think of a time when you may have feigned illness or injury. Why are we sometimes reluctant to "be healed?"
*What is the difference between **denying** suffering, **dwelling** in suffering, and **dealing** with suffering?*

CHAPTER ELEVEN:
THE FALSE JOY OF EMPTY RELIGION

"For there is one God and one mediator between
God and mankind, the man Christ Jesus"
(1 Timothy 2:5)

I was once able to tour the ruins of Herculaneum in Italy — a sister city to Pompeii that was also buried in the volcanic eruption of Mount Vesuvius in 79 AD. Walking through streets and houses frozen in time, I noticed a number of amphorae, or empty jars, that had once been used for storing food and wine. It got me thinking — I wonder if they found any empty jars in the kitchens of the temples?

Over time I've observed that church kitchens are a grave-yard for **empty containers.** Years of potlucks, wedding receptions, and funerals supply most houses of worship with shelves that overflow with forgotten casserole dishes, bowls and plasticware containers (but never the lids for some reason).

Did ancient Apollo worshippers have the same problem? Did they have "temple workdays" where forgotten, empty jars and bowls were tossed out? Have congregations in all places and times struggled with the blight of empty containers?

The irony cuts thick when we consider that religion itself has a tendency to become an empty container.

You may have heard the clever saying that Christianity is not a religion but a relationship. I agree wholeheartedly with the intent of that saying. It is true — but it's also an oversimplification.

Let's back up a moment and look at the roots of the word "religion". It comes from the Latin *"religare,"* which very simply means *"to bind"* or *"hold together."*

It's the basis of many modern words — *ligament*, for example, which binds muscle to bone, and *ligature,* which can refer to the stitching a surgeon uses to bind and heal the body.

Thus, the concept of "religion", at its heart, refers to the binding together of God and man — and, more specifically, the **means** by which that bond takes place.

In another sense, we could compare religion to a container, much like the vessels we use for "holding together" food and drink. Those containers are important — we could even argue that they are necessary. Imagine a grocery store without containers — what would the salad dressing aisle look like?

Because we live in a material world, even something as ethereal as spirituality requires at least some sort of "container" to be made manifest in our daily lives. Those containers might be as rudimentary as language, as in the words of a song or prayer; or they might be as elaborate as an ornate house of worship where people can gather protected from the rain and "be spiritual".

The problem comes when we pay homage to the container and ignore the contents.

I know a man who owns a $46,000 bottle of wine. Of course he would never drink the wine — it is a collector's item. But suppose one day he did ... *would that empty bottle be worth anything?*

Not really. I suppose he might keep the bottle on a shelf somewhere as a reminder of what it once stood for. Tourists might take selfies in front of it eventually. But devoid of wine, the container is worth next to nothing.

In the end, a container is only as valuable as its contents.

Casting for God

Most religious effort amounts to the absurdity of a person who has fallen overboard attempting to throw a lifeline to their rescue boat.

Throughout history, humanity has developed various "containers" and "ligatures" to attempt to reconnect with a distant god or gods. We've developed special rituals, magic spells, and even bloody sacrifices — all man-made attempts to reconnect with God, as though we could somehow cast a line far enough to snag Heaven.

If, however, as the Scriptures teach, humanity is **hopelessly** fallen while God is **infinitely** perfect, human beings can cast no line long enough to save themselves. We are working from the bottom of a bottomless pit. And yet we keep trying by engaging in religious rituals that might give us a little boost, but ultimately take us nowhere.

In classic Christianity, we are not to harbor such delusions. The beauty of the way of Christ is that God reaches out to rescue us, and not the other way around. The tie that binds God to man was not braided by human hands but by the love of God. The lifeline of Jesus is sent down from above. In Christ, we no longer need to launch the paper kites of religious works Heavenward in a futile attempt to reach God, for God has extended Himself to reach us. Jesus is our ligature, the ladder that reconnects us with the Father and offers real hope.

The difference between Christian religion and all others is the binding agent: other religions depend on human-crafted routines and rituals, man-made ladders and ligatures to reach God. Christians believe that **God Himself** provided the means of our reconnection in the person of Jesus Christ. In the Christian faith, **Jesus alone is the stairway to Heaven** — the only true ligament that can reconnect the muscle of Heaven to our weary bones.

Authentic Christian worship is not a collection of human attempts to reach God but a celebration of what **God** has already done to **reach us**. The point of Christian prayer is not to **bargain** with God, rather to **surrender** to His grace; not to toss flimsy threads upward but to grasp the thick rope which He has already lowered.

James 1:27 tells us that *"Religion that God our Father accepts as pure and faultless is this: to look after orphans and widows in their distress and to keep oneself from being polluted by the world."*

Good religion, then, reconnects with God simply by going where He goes; participating in His work — looking after "widows and orphans in their distress," and keeping ourselves "from being polluted by the world." **Good religion**, as the practice of both **doing good** and **being good**, is a worthy container for a rich spiritual life. Unlike the emptiness of bad religion, this kind of religion brings us great joy as our lives resonate with the purposes of God.

Empty religion, on the other hand, is joyless. It pushes a dusty, dogmatic, and decaying set of rituals meant to manipulate and control God rather than liberate the soul in Christ.

Now, I can guess what my more free-church, protestant friends are thinking. Perhaps they are falsely assuming that I'm taking aim at our more liturgical brethren. Not so! I've discovered the joy of fellowship with immensely committed and vibrant followers of Jesus Christ in both high- and low-church settings. We don't have to agree on every point of doctrine in order to be bound together by the way of Christ.

What's more, in my experience, free-church dogma can run just as deep as high-church dogma. My less-liturgical brothers and sisters might think that they are free from the bondage of man-made traditions, but every group of faithful believers, without exception, falls into the trap of routines that can become dogmatic over time.

For example, as a young man I once met a retired missionary who wore an unusually large wooden cross around his neck. He explained to me how his cross was the "right" cross because Jesus wasn't depicted on it. *I hadn't noticed it before, but someone had taken Jesus off all the crosses in my church!*

As a kid who had grown up Roman Catholic before personally reconnecting with Christ in the context of a less formal church setting, I had been fascinated by the suffering depicted on crucifixes. It didn't seem like such a bad thing to me to remember what the Lord went through. The thorns, the rip in His ribs, the somehow peaceful anguish depicted on His face. These painted a potent picture of the price Jesus paid for love.

But this retired missionary proceeded to lay out his protestant dogma: "Why would anyone wear a cross that depicts a dead Jesus when He is no longer dead, but alive?" he asked me.

I could see his point. But I also wondered, "Well then, why wear the cross at all? Why not wear an emblem of an empty tomb instead, with a tiny little Jesus smiling and waving as He exits? Wouldn't that be more accurate?"

I'm sure that gentleman meant well, but he was the first of many free-church Christians I've met over the years who are just as dogmatic on mostly debatable issues as some of our more liturgical counterparts.

Everyone, no matter how sincerely they start out, is not only *capable* of allowing heart-religion to devolve into dogma but downright *prone* to it. Even self-proclaimed "non-religious" people can be quite dogmatic.

This is true in nearly every walk of life I've encountered. Baseball players have a home plate ritual. Star Trek fans have ritualized Vulcan greetings and hand signals. Even Dead Heads have their own code. Consider the tremendous religion-like grit it requires for our atheist friends to insist that *nothing* begot *everything*!

Again, I want to emphasize this: all religion is not necessarily a bad thing. The Bible teaches us that religion can be good, pure and faultless. But religion certainly has a tendency to devolve into petty dogma in a big hurry, and that is what we must avoid, for there is no joy in it.

Joy Restored: Reconciliation with God

When we're feeling disconnected from God, what we need is reconnection, not empty religion. It may be temporarily soothing to adopt the comforting routines of paint-by-number religion, but rituals by themselves will not bring us lasting joy. Joy is found in reconnecting with God by being reconciled to Him through Christ, not in carving deeper religious ruts.

Rituals cannot heal a broken heart, only the Lord can do that. Rote prayers and strict routines might distract us for a time, temporarily taking our minds off of our suffering, but if God is not at the center of them, they will not produce joy.

The Scriptures teach us that we are all fallen and in need of salvation. This salvation cannot be wrought by any human power — not by ourselves, not by any priest, and not by any pastor.

The apostle Peter famously preached to the religious leaders of his day:

> *"Jesus is 'the stone you builders rejected,*
> *which has become the cornerstone.'*
> *Salvation is found in no one else,*
> *for there is no other name under heaven given to mankind*
> *by which we must be saved."*
> *(Acts 4:12)*

Only Jesus can restore unto us the joy of salvation. No one else but the blameless Son of God could take up the cross as a substitute offering for our sin. No one else is qualified. It took a spotless sin offering, an innocent lamb, a sinless sacrifice. Pastors, popes, and the psychic down the street would hardly choose to stand in our place on the cross.

But Jesus did.

The only one who could unlock the joy of salvation and reconciliation with God is the Word made flesh, Heaven's ligature, the Lord Jesus Christ. Paul heartily agrees with Peter when he writes:

> *"For there is one God and one mediator*
> *between God and mankind,*
> *the man Christ Jesus."*
> *(1 Timothy 2:5).*

We are set free from the bonds of bad religion by a simple relationship with Jesus. Only a relationship with the Son can usher us into the glory of the Father's presence. Only in Christ are the old wounds healed for certain. Only in Jesus do we make peace with our past. Only by grace, mediated by the Lamb of God, can we enter into the incomparable joy of being present to God.

If God has already done all the work of salvation, what is left for us to do? Simply take hold of the rope. Cling to Jesus.

> *"If you declare with your mouth, 'Jesus is Lord,'*
> *and believe in your heart*
> *that God raised him from the dead,*
> *you will be saved."*
> *(Romans 10:9)*

No magic spell. No altar call. No rosary. No Sunday School class. No special pilgrimage. Simply confess our need and hold on to Jesus.

False Mediators

If Jesus is the one true mediator appointed by God, there also must be false mediators. What follows are just a few I've learned to watch out for.

Trinkets and Touchstones

When I travel, I like to pick up a magnet to put on my fridge at home. They are touchstones that help preserve memories that I might otherwise soon forget.

In the world of religion, touchstones abound. On a recent trip to Jerusalem, I was determined to pick up no more than one or two fridge magnets. But as anyone who's been to that city can tell you, that's not so easy. Walking the Via Dolorosa, I was inundated with street hawkers, offering enough souvenirs to open my own flea market. Everything from "real" widow's mites to sacred shot glasses are thrust upon would-be pilgrims in the holy city.

It isn't just **items** that hold special significance for us, though. **Places** can also remind us of the things God has done. Jews, Muslims and Christians alike flock to Palestine with a devout religious fervor, eager to pray where David might have prayed, to pray where Mohammed might have prayed, and to "walk where Jesus walked."

While there is nothing necessarily wrong with personal reminders and touchstones that remind us of the things God has done in the past, we are in danger of crossing into the waters of bad religion when we worship the touchstone rather than the God they represent. Even worse is when we prescribe our personal touchstones as requirements for other people to observe. This is what bad religion does — it takes a simple, useful remembrance and elevates it into a sacrament that everyone must revere, even if it means nothing to them personally.

Of course, Jesus endorsed two particular touchstones to help remind us and the world of His ministry. However, they are simple and few; scour the New Testament, and you will discover that communion and baptism are the only two sacraments Jesus specifically told His followers to observe.

Beyond those, all else is optional. Other touchstones may be meaningful to us, and even draw us closer to God — but they can also very easily become distractions from God. More than that, we should avoid foisting the observance of our own personal touchstone on others for whom they will have little or no meaning.

So, I will keep my Jerusalem fridge magnet — but only as long as it serves the purpose of aiding in remembrance. Once trinkets and touchstones become the objects of affection themselves, we've gone off the range. Sacramentalism quickly devolves into the joyless practice of idolatry.

"They have thrown their gods into the fire
and destroyed them, for they were not gods
but only wood and stone,
fashioned by human hands."
(2 Kings 19:18)

Opulent Words and Sanctimonious Speech

Do you know where the stage magic words "hocus pocus" come from? There is a bit of speculation, but one of the most likely explanations is that it originally was a play on words from the old Latin mass when the priest would lift the bread and quote Jesus at the last supper: "Hoc est corpus meum," or "This is my body."

Hoc est corpus ... Hocus pocus ...

Presto! Bread becomes flesh!

Most of us don't speak Latin, but I do notice that all religious people tend to rely heavily on "magic words" to pepper their prayers and public speech — not "abracadabra" or "hocus pocus," but perhaps words that can become just as empty.

One variety of "magic words" used by Christians is the awkward use of terms of endearment for God in public prayer. For some believers, phrases like "Abba Father" or "Father God" are often repeated like punctuation at the beginning and end of every sentence.

Some of the most devout believers I know pray this way — I don't mean to diminish their intent, and I certainly don't question their sincerity. But I must confess that it feels unnatural to speak this way to a friend.

It could be my raised-religious hang-ups, too. As someone who grew up reciting rote prayers as a daily discipline, I may just be oversensitive to lofty-sounding prayers. But I do wonder if we aren't sometimes slipping into a practice akin to reciting incantations to try to curry favor with God when we pray this way. Perhaps a simpler, more conversational approach to prayer is better.

Another breed of "magic words" we sometimes hear among people who believe in Jesus is what someone once cleverly labeled "Christianese" — words and phrases that are particular to the context of Christianity, but don't make sense anywhere else.

For example, in the context in which I currently serve, it is not uncommon to hear a certain word — a very good word, but very often misunderstood, if understood at all. The word is "sanctification," and it basically means surrendering our lives to Christ.

But relatively few people know what to do with that word, or other words like "justification," "redemption," and even such a key word as "salvation." We keep saying these words, but to our hearers, I do not think they mean what we think they mean.

There are other more comical examples: I once heard of a clearly well-meaning Christian, who was praying with someone, encouraging them to "Just hang on" and then "Just let go!"

Two, obviously heartfelt and good sentiments, but without knowing the context, they made no sense.

Language is a funny thing. Open language helps us communicate with one another, and that is good. But exclusive language always excludes others.

What good is it if we speak code and no one has a decoder ring?

I know a man who is afraid to pray in public because he is not eloquent like the elders of his church. Their prayers often soar in platitudes of "thees" and "thous" and all manner of lofty phraseology. When an opportunity arises for public prayer, my friend hides his face and prays privately that he won't be called on. He is ashamed that he does not know how to pray with great style and flair around others.

However, I know my friend prays inwardly constantly talking to the Lord as casually as a good friend. I know God hears him when he prays. No magic words, just heartfelt love for his savior.

"And when you pray, do not keep on babbling like pagans, for they think they will be heard because of their many words." (Matthew 6:7)

Surrogates and Stand-Ins

It's human nature to idolize the people we respect. Whether they are sports heroes, celebrities, family members, or leaders, it is difficult to resist the temptation to add unnecessary and unwarranted weight to the opinions of those we admire. Instead of asking, "What would Jesus do?" we ask ourselves, "What would

Billy Graham do?"

Religions are inordinately concerned with titles and status. In some circles, it is anathema to call the pastor by their first name. In others, the pastor's wife must always be called "The First Lady." I have heard an alarming statistic that a near majority of seminary students today are entering the ministry primarily so that they may have the title of "Pastor" or "Doctor."

Woe to the body of Christ if that is the case!

Every one of us has a God shaped hole that only God can fill, but that doesn't stop us from trying to fill it with other surrogate Messiahs. Maybe it's your mom. Maybe it's a favorite preacher or other Christian celebrity. Maybe it is the person who led you to the Lord. Regardless of the person it may be in each of our lives, we have to remember that there is only one mediator between God and man. There is nothing wrong with respecting and listening to our mothers or a Christian teacher — as long as we don't put them on the pedestal that is reserved for God alone. We must be careful to avoid putting any human being in a position only suited for God.

"And do not call anyone on earth 'father,' for you have one Father, and he is in heaven." (Matthew 23:9)

The Truth that Sets us Free

Joy is not found in empty religion. It is found in reconciliation with God. And thanks be to God, the hardest work of reconciliation has already been done by Jesus Christ.

> *"If you declare with your mouth,*
> *'Jesus is Lord,' and believe in your heart*
> *that God raised him from the dead,*
> *you will be saved."*
> *(Romans 10:9)*

No physical trinkets, no opulent words, no surrogate Messiahs. Just Jesus. All we need to do is believe and follow Him. Let us cast aside empty religion and be reconciled to God the Father

through Christ the Son.
True joy is found in no one else.

For Discussion:
Have you ever had a "good luck charm"?
Why are humans drawn to idols?
What makes God better than any idol?

Chapter Twelve:
The False Joy of Self-Worship

"For by the grace given to me I say to everyone among you
not to think of himself more highly than he ought to think,
but to think with sober judgment,
each according to the measure of faith
that God has assigned."
(Romans 12:3)

I recently read about a woman cited for calling 911 three times to report that her local McDonald's had run out of Chicken McNuggets, claiming it was an "emergency." I don't know how true that story is, but it does highlight one of our society's greatest problems: ***self-centeredness*** — what I will call ***the false joy of self-worship.***

In today's culture, it is always "me first." Selfishness pervades every aspect of our lives. From entertainment to politics to education to religion, one god seems to reign supreme: the god of self — that's you and me, the consumers of stuff. We worship retailers promising to feed our every whim. Politicians preach crowd-pleasing sermons to scratch our itching ears, making vows no one can keep.

There is only one lord in most of our lives, and it is that suspicious character known as "me." Most of us worship the self — *the ego*. If I want something, I must have it — *now*. If I don't get enough attention, I walk away from the relationship. If I don't get what I want when I want it, I call a lawyer and demand retribution.

We have created a society where every person among us thinks and acts as though they are their own god. Commercialism thrives on this idolatry, and so, unfortunately, does religion.

Observe how more and more churches are geared toward *our* personal comfort, *our* expectation for entertainment, and *our* desire not to be inconvenienced by any difficult truth or significant spiritual expectation of responsibility. Churches have become fawningly *seeker-centric* and just barely *Spirit-sensitive*, rather than seeking to be simply *seeker-sensitive* while remaining fervently *Christ-centered*.

The body of Christ remains just as guilty of idolatry as the children of Israel who danced around the golden calf. In our case, however, the false gods we dance to please are the people who enter our doors rather than the one true God.

Do we think that such selfish, ego-driven living has produced true, lasting joy? Certainly not. As we swell our heads with notions of our own divinity, we set ourselves up to pop miserably when the reality of our own frailty sets in. No human being can bear the tremendous strain of being a god, but that is precisely what we have come to expect of ourselves in this age of egocentric self-worship.

Looking for joy in our selfishness, we have found only the bitterness of depression. Seeking personal satisfaction, each self-serving heart finds itself only aching for something more.

Good News: We're Not God

Of course, it doesn't have to be this way. A pathway to true joy exists if we are brave enough to abandon selfishness and declare that we are *not* God, *not* the center of the universe, and that there is a reality more real than what our senses can detect.

From the beginning, God — *the real God who exists beyond our tiny self-concept* — has desired that we experience true and lasting joy, not by worshiping ourselves but by worshiping Him. When our self-conceptions are aligned with His conceptions of us, we find the tremendously liberating truth that we are not the center of the universe. God is.

Egocentricity is ultimately limited and dissatisfying, while *theocentricity* — putting God at the center — is where lasting joy begins.

In the Scriptures, this deification of ego, or worship of the self, is given a special name: *pride.*

An example is in Proverbs 16:18, where we read that, *"Pride goes before destruction"* and in 1 John 2:16,

> *"For all that is in the world — the desires of the flesh and the desires of the eyes and pride of life — is not from the Father but is from the world."*

This misguided pride is also referred to in the Scriptures as arrogance, haughtiness, and vanity. (It is not to be confused with the healthy and appropriate pride a parent feels for a growing child.)

The Scriptures reveal that selfish pride is the root of all sin and, therefore, the source of all disappointment in life. Egocentricity, self-service, arrogance, vanity — all names for sinful pride — bring only *temporary joy.* Lasting joy comes when we surrender our pride and find our worth in Christ.

Romans 12:3 challenges us not to think of ourselves with arrogant pride, but *"to think with sober judgment, each according to the measure of faith that God has assigned."*

The cure for sinful pride (and thus the key to lasting joy) is to find our value *in the way that God measures our value* rather than in boosting our own egos with false measures of pride. In other words, we find the truest joy when we reckon our worth according to God's declaration of our worth rather than our own cooked up, conflated conceptions.

Wait a minute — we may be thinking, "This is too risky. What if God doesn't like me as much as I like myself? What if I don't agree with the value God assigns me? Why would I put all my eggs in that basket and risk being disappointed? What if God lets me down?"

If you are asking these questions, I'd like to share glad tidings of great joy: God's estimation of us far exceeds our own estimation of ourselves.

While we're at it, God's *love* for us far exceeds our own love of ourselves.

And God's desire to bring us lasting joy far exceeds our ability to boost joy on our own.

And so, we come to three areas where I believe we each must surrender control and hand it over to God. I am certain there are others, but I would like to propose that, if we can relinquish our control in these three areas, we will discover lasting joy that comes — not from egocentric selfishness — but from selfless, God-centered living.

God-Righteous versus Self-Righteous

The ego loves to declare its own righteousness, but we know that no one is truthfully righteous. Take the guy who won't stop for directions as an example. Why do we insist we are right when we are obviously lost? The book of Proverbs reminds us that, *"There is a way that seems right to a man, but its end is the way to death." (Proverbs 14:12)*

The antidote for self-righteousness is God-righteousness.

Here's what I mean: a guilty defendant can declare herself innocent as much as she likes, but it means nothing **until the judge declares her so.**

Let's stop pretending we're perfect and recognize that, apart from God's declaration of our innocence through the atoning blood of Jesus Christ, we are a mess. If our ego declares us righteous, it means very little. But if God declares us righteous, we are righteous indeed!

"Therefore, as one trespass led to condemnation for all men, so one act of righteousness leads to justification and life for all men." (Romans 5:8)

God-Important versus Self-Important

We all want to know that our lives mean something, that we are important, that we matter — but as life goes on, most of us will discover the painful truth that we are, indeed, very small. We may convince ourselves of our own importance, but time will, unfortunately, prove us wrong. Even the most famous among us will be forgotten soon enough. While some of us may find importance for a moment, it will be fleeting, leaving our egos scrambling to find a way to be "important" again.

Fortunately, while the world will forget everything about us, God will not. In fact, even as the world passes us by, the Scriptures promise that we each are very important to God. He thinks about us. He knows us. He is mindful of us. Psalm 8:4 reminds us of our God-importance: *"What is man that you are mindful of him, and the son of man that you care for him?"*

God indeed cares for each one of us. Our longing for importance is met fully when we rest in the shadow of His wing.

God-Validated versus Self-Validated

Have you ever tried to leave a parking lot without ticket validation? It can be an expensive experience!

Even more painful is going through life with the aching sense that we, ourselves, are not valid. Based on this deep insecurity, many of us make attempts to self-validate by winning accolades and proving ourselves to our neighbors. But the final exit toll doesn't accept self-validated tickets. For many of us, our insecurity runs so deep that we can never quite earn the validation we so desperately crave, and we languish with only the false joys of trophies and sheepskins to comfort us.

In Christ, however, we find that our seemingly invalidating weaknesses become our greatest allies, for only when we are found to be weak in our own strength can the strength of God begin to work full force. When we pursue the false joy of self-validation, we will always come up short. But when we lay our insecurities at the foot of the cross, we find that Jesus has been waiting for us to surrender all along. Then, when we are finally ready to admit our weakness, He can be our strength.

"But he said to me, 'My grace is sufficient for you,
for my power is made perfect in weakness.'

Therefore I will boast all the more gladly of my weaknesses,
so that the power of Christ may rest upon me."
(2 Corinthians 12:9)

When we are in Christ, we are valid in God's eyes. We are important in God's sight. And, although it may seem like the suit is too big to wear, we are even righteous according to His measurement.

Ego-Prioritization, Not Ego-Annihilation

By attacking egocentricity, I'm not advocating for annihilation of the self, merely the *reprioritization* of the self. Our egos are healthiest when they are not the center of our existence. God doesn't want to *destroy* our sense of self — rather, in Christ He wants to *elevate* each of us to a plane we could never reach *on our own*. We find our joy when we prioritize God as the center, not ourselves.

The Courage to Surrender

The search for joy in the deserts of egocentricity and self-ishness is ultimately futile. We must find the courage to lay our egos in the hands of Jesus if we want to find joy that never fails.

True joy comes when we do not need to be the main actor on stage. True joy comes when we realize that we were never in the starring role to begin with. We find freedom when we are not the center of the universe.

Either He must be Lord, or me.

If it is me, woe is me.

If it is Him, unspeakable joy awaits!

For Discussion:
If God believes everyone is worth dying for, what does that say about our worth?
Can you think of someone who thinks of themselves too highly?
*What is the difference between **healthy self-care** and **unhealthy self-worship**?*

Acknowledgements

So many friends to thank!

To all of those who have offered ideas, thank you for your insight and willingness to share your personal struggle to reclaim holy joy in the midst of suffering and uncertainty.

I owe special thanks to Paige O'Neal's weekly Bible Study group at Spring Valley Community Church, Ed and Kathi Poole's *Porch Sunday School Class* and the guys of my church's *Friday Morning Fellas Fellowship* for offering intriguing suggestions to consider in this series of sermons.

I also owe deep thanks to my friends who write so well for providing feedback and suggestions as editors. In alphabetical order: Natalie Jager, Lauren Mix, Kathi Poole and Brooke Yeider. Your corrections were invaluable. Your thoughts and ideas were brilliant! Thank you. I cannot tell you how much I appreciate you.

To Cindy Hoffman and Kristen Hetrick — thank you for sharing your thoughts, but most of all for sharing the joy of your children. They will always remain in my heart.

I must thank my dear friends Pastor Scott and Rhonda Archer for their undying support and encouragement over the past quarter century. Tammie and I are thankful to God for the community of joy God has provided through your friendship. We are much more than blessed by you!

My children, Cambria, James, John — and now Nathan Judd — thank you for bringing me joy in a million ways you will likely never know.

Not least of all: to my wife Tammie — thank you for your steadfast encouragement and comfort. You still amaze me.

May the grace of our Lord be with you, now and always!

Pastor Steve Babbitt
Spring Valley, CA
February 2022

ABOUT THE AUTHOR

Steve Babbitt is Senior Pastor at Spring Valley Community Church in San Diego, California. Steve regularly speaks at events and is available for retreats, conferences and workshops as a presenter and panelist. Contact him at stevebab@cox.net.

Made in the USA
Middletown, DE
20 November 2022

15069305R00073